D0097373

EFFING SIMPLE

BY

TONI VANSCHOYCK

EFFING SIMPLE

DREAMSTARTERS

www.DreamStartersPublishing.com

Acknowledgements

I (we) have so many people to thank, but for time purposes, there are some that absolutely need to be mentioned, because they made this possible.

First and foremost, to my network marketing family thank you, thank you, thank you. Without the **Urdenatas**, this would not be possible. Especially to Sr. Luis for that first crucial time we met and he challenged me to dream bigger.

To **Ray**—you lead with such integrity and I am proud to call you a mentor and friend. Thank you for continuing to lead the way and show us what is possible.

To **Stuart MacMillian**, thank you for being real and honest and pushing us (me) to be better.

Lu and Javier, thank you for all of the wonderful contributions you made to create and grow one of the greatest companies. This work is truly legendary!
To our team and family, I love all of you so much. Please know that working with you and the aforementioned made this possible. I don't know if this would have been published without all of you. Mandi Schroers, Anne Fisher, Amy Lazare, Amy Campos, Jackie Boelke, Jennifer Pavlick, Phyllis Benstein, Tammy Causley, Suzanne Krygier, Kristi Heinz, Becki Burke, Gem Medrano, and the other two Miami 11 Jewely Stephens and Kyla Williamson, and the future leaders of Team Tri-umph, thank you, thank you, thank you!!

To my dear friend and mentor **Natalie Richardson**, I owe you so much for your invaluable advice! Love ya lady!

To just a few friends that have influenced us so much; **Amanda & Dave Barrett** (photo cred to Amanda she rocks), Roxy Henley, Rachel and Ryan Lee, Susette & Don Andrews and Andra Reynolds thank you for always cheering us on!

Thank you to the Universe for aligning the path to make this happen.

I have three incredible people that made this book come to life on paper: **Mike Fallat, Melissa Drake and Lisa Dove**.

Most of all of my family **Jay, Naomi, and Catherine** LOVE YOU!!

And one last shout to is to my dad—thank you for my work ethic. You taught me how to work and go after everything you love! Thanks to you, I'm doing it!

Even though I could only mention a few folks, there are thousands more. You know who you are…Here's a big thanks to you as well. I love y'all!,

Most of this book has the how to's keeping it light and funny and I pray that you will find value in it. Writing this first book has been scary, a lot of time and heart into it. If some of the language offends you I won't apologize it is the authentic me.

Foreword

Just like the book's title, Toni Vanschoyck grabs your attention. With her no-nonsense approach to business, she has a knack for cutting through the minutiae and focusing on the fundamentals. She's seen the good, the bad and the ugly in this industry and has mastered the art of turning set*backs* into a set*up* for growth and success. What truly makes her special, though, is her genuine desire to help others grow and succeed in ways they never could have imagined for themselves. This book is just one example of her commitment to inspiring others while reminding them that this business really Is. That. Simple. Stop letting things be so difficult and read this book… you'll be effing glad you did!

Natalie Richardson
Regional Sales Director, Certified Coach DSWA

Table of Contents

Foreword 53

Introduction 7

Effing Simple Why 10

Effing Simple Energy 25

Effing Simple Drama Ditch 42

Effing Simple Thirst 50

Effing Simple Partnerships 61

Effing Simple Re-purpose 76

Effing Simple Environment 85

Effing Simple Onboarding or Recruitment Process 94

Effing Simple Servant Leadership 117

Effing Simple Profession 129

Effing Simple Social Media/Marketing

Effing Great Product 140

Effing Simple Training 148

Effing Simple Presentation 156

Introduction

This book is about network marketing and leadership. Even though these pages are focused on network marketing, the tips I outline are going to hold true for anyone who is in a retail position, is a business owner, or anything in between. More importantly, this book is for **dreamers**—people who know what they want and want to know how to get there.

If your dreams don't scare you, they're not big enough! says my 11-year-old daughter, Catherine.

I am living proof that you can achieve your dream—without sacrificing your family, your happiness, and your life. I was the first market partner with my current network marketing company. I lead a team of more than 200,000 partners who generate a whopping 85% of the sales for this company. This is a massive organization on its way to a billion dollars in annual sales.

You can achieve this type of success.

Yes on the surface, this book is about business lessons. But, the principles here can be applied to life. It's effing simple, and I'll be there to help you through it all. Anything we talk about here you can bring into your life; your family relationships, friendships, and your relationship with yourself.

I started in network marketing twenty years ago, and six companies ago—and I sucked at it! I bounced from product to product, company to company, and just didn't have a groove. In fact, before I got started in network marketing, I was dead-set against it. I thought it was a scam. You know, that stupid clichéd saying "pyramid?" And you were expected to recruit all your friends and family into a pyramid scheme. I was afraid of what people would say about me.

But I didn't know what I didn't know. Fortunately, I had a really good friend, and one of our best landscaping clients. She started in a personal care products company and invited me to attend an informational meeting. I really resisted, but she offered me wine (well duh). I needed to go because she was such a great supporter of our business. I went, and I got schooled—believe me. It was an a-ha serendipitous epiphany.

I signed up on the spot and did mediocre for about six months—then things really stagnated. Because I didn't really know how to work a networking business. I also had no idea that this industry is about other people, not me. I was never really taught how to build a strong, growing network. I was basically told, "Just make a list of people you know, and keep on bugging them," instead of being taught how to grow your list and network. You can't rely on the same 10, 20, or 30 people all the time.

In 2014, after only working for my current company for a month, I'll never forget the day I got my first check. We were in our backyard, in a town home community, when FedEx pulled up to the house. Jay, my husband, came back and told me, "Hey, you have something here." I opened the envelope and screamed when I saw that I had made $8,900 in my first 10 days!!! I jumped up and down, screaming, "This is it, this is it...it's going to work!" I'm sure my neighbors thought I was headed to the looney bin—but, you know what? I knew in that moment, I made the right decision. I've never looked back.

I finally figured things out, it is silly simple, effing simple and I'm hoping I can save you twenty years or less of struggling, by learning from my ineptitude.

So, let's get effing started! ***It's just effing simple.***

Chapter 1

Effing Simple *Why*

When creating a business for yourself, it always comes down to your "**Why**."

If you've ever spent time around kids, you've been subjected to the most classic and sometimes constant childhood inquiries. You know the ones I'm talking about; every single question begins with "Why?"

Even from a young age, we know intuitively the motive behind an action is the most important piece of every story. *Starting and growing a business to an epic level is no different—it begins with the question, "Why?"* In some ways, I think this type of business is an ongoing life, self-awareness course. Your "why" will help you understand more about yourself than just about anything else you can do. You can create **and** find yourself. You can create brand new behaviors and habits because you're always learning when you start on the adventure of having your own business.

Since finding my "why" and engaging in network marketing, I'm a different person than I was. I'm convinced that if it were not for my career in network marketing, I would still be a bitter, single bitch. I love myself so much better now. I can remember certain conversations I would have, and recall all the negativity spewing out of my mouth. I didn't like that person I was. Uncovering my "why" helped me make changes in my life that I never thought possible.

There are many reasons why people become entrepreneurs. Some of the most common reasons include personal satisfaction, creative independence, and/or financial stability. Usually, the main motivator is money, but sometimes people are afraid to admit that because they'll be looked at as "greedy." So, it's more important to dive in to explore what it is that you really need. Draw those bigger goals out—I call them BHAGs—Big Hairy Audacious (or Ass) Goals.

Let me get something out here, right from the start. We have been trained in our society to look down on wealth. We are afraid to even write down having money as a goal. That's bullshit! That's society saying, "Ok, you need to be with the status quo—you need to be mediocre—and, if you have money, you're a bad person."

Just recently, we booked our first family vacation together. I can't tell you the satisfaction I felt when I reserved the 25,000 square foot Airbnb property on a beach in Saint Barth, and casually clicked the "reserve" button, watched the money instantly come out of the debit card, and didn't think twice. That's the kind of BHAG I'm talking about! Having the ability to go anywhere and do anything—that is effing freedom!!

Women, especially, often don't address their own needs. When we think of goals, we tend to think of our own family, or our parents, or others we can help. When I got started in this industry, one of my initial goals was just to have a shoe fund! Plus, being able to go to Whole Foods and drop money on healthy food, because back then, grocery shopping at Whole Foods took my whole pay check.

Digging deeper into that goal, and we see that a primary reason people start their own businesses can be summed up in one word—FREEDOM. You will be hearing this effing word a lot (and yes, you can start singing George Michael).

Freedom can come in many different forms: the freedom to set your own schedule, the freedom to work wherever you want, and the freedom to make medical and other appointments (for yourself—and your family) without worrying about depleting sick and vacation time. Freedom also shows up when you pick your children up after school, volunteer at mid-week, mid-day holiday school parties, and even consider home-schooling or hiring a private tutor for your children so your family can travel freely, without being tied to a school schedule and location.

Abundance in your life is having a balance between faith, family, friends, finances and fitness. Money does great things. I've learned, people can be assholes without money, and with money. I hope part of what I teach you in this book is how to get over this fear of making money, because suddenly you'll be a "bad person." Wipe that shit out of your head. It is the number one thing holding you back.

A *huge* component of having a strong inner-game is having a powerful "Why" that moves you forward.

I actually have two. My primary "Why" is my family, and my secondary "Why" is the ability to change lives. I feel like one of my primary life purposes is to help people see their potential, and network marketing just happens to be a great avenue to do that. Plus, it's really good money!

I want to inspire you, motivate you, and teach you that if you can just change two things a day that you're doing, it will forever change your life. And, trust me, I've seen people struggle with this, until they get involved in this industry, and then it's like someone hit them over the head with a rock.

For me, family is first. And some family is not blood related.

I was born into a family that was struggling. My dad went to night school and was studying for exams to earn his MBA. Back then, that piece of paper meant much more than it does now. He had a hell of a work ethic and loved what he did. I truly believe I learned that from him. He was always striving to do and be better (for himself and for his family).

Eventually, he was running companies—*big ones.* As a family, we had everything; including nice cars, nice homes, and every luxury we wanted. Except, my dad was never home to enjoy these things with us. For me, his absence put a damper on his "success" and left a bad taste in my mouth.

I was always a rebel. I learned early on that I wanted to make it on my own. I knew I was destined for something amazing. It's always been important for me to do things on my own terms.

Also, hearing the word "No" feels like a challenge to me. When people tell me no, I often feel compelled to respond with, "Watch me, bitches!" I'm quite tenacious, and persistent—especially when it comes to things that are near and dear to me; like my family.

At the young age of 15, I started working by busing tables for a fast food chain. I worked every chance I got. While my peers were going out on weekends, I was working. I worked my way from a local chain restaurant to some upscale establishments because the tips at the high-end restaurants were better.

Eventually, when it was time for college, my father offered to pay my tuition at the University of Michigan. GO BLUE! While my dad paid the tuition, I was responsible to pay my living expenses. During this time, I had my first child and my first divorce. Little did I know then that I was on the Liz Taylor plan (for the record, I didn't marry an ex-spouse). I was a young single mother, but I knew I could make it work because I had developed a strong work ethic as a teenager. Now, I am passing this drive and skill on to my children while building a legacy.

After finishing college, I went into the corporate restaurateur side of the business, working day and night. As if navigating my work hours wasn't challenging enough, I also travelled occasionally for work. My schedule and availability were not conducive to raising a family—especially as a single mother. However, I managed to stick out this pace for six years. All the while, I was damn tired and my family connections suffered.

As a mom, volleying day care just sucked—you know how expensive that is, right? I did not want my children in day care. When I remarried, I had two more babies while starting a business in landscaping and having a home-based day care. The cost of caring for my children and the demands of motherhood helped me realize that I am definitely not a 9 to 5 gal. I needed the freedom to create my own schedule, and to spend as much time with my children as possible. A corporate job dictates schedules—and while some people thrive on that, some—like 'moi'—don't.

While in the landscaping business, I managed the schedule, but I was a slave to mother nature. Basically, it is feast or famine in landscaping! When things were good, they were really good. But, if the weather was bad (as it often is in the northern Midwest), there was no income. Balance and budgetary concerns were a constant struggle. As one who worked the land, the gains in freedom from a crushing workload equaled a loss in financial stability. The day care business offset some of that roller coaster, but it still wasn't enough. I was miserable. We worked seven days a week in the summer. The hours were long and went well past dusk for three to four months straight. Worse, we didn't get to enjoy the few months of decent weather because we were working in it.

I knew I had to get off of the roller coaster. It wasn't worth it.

Five years later, with three babies in tow, my second husband left. Once again, I was a single mom. Completely terrified, I wondered how I would provide for my three children. Day care costs were a serious concern. Yet, I was determined not to leave my children with strangers. Plus, the expense was beyond my means. At the same time, I was unfulfilled in the corporate world.

When I started my journey in network marketing, the 2008 recession hit close to home. When "The Big Three" (Ford, GM, and Chrysler) nearly collapsed and restructured, many people lost their jobs. This led to cutbacks in all areas—

especially in discretionary spending. As a result, our income was severely cut.

That's when I was enlightened. Actually, it was more like being hit in the head with a brick, but the effect was the same.

Enlightenment showed me the way my businesses were susceptible to the larger economy and how network marketing enabled me to supplement the business income through product sales.

A year and a half later, feeling like a Liz Taylor protege, I was on relationship number three and baby number four. The stakes were high for me and Jay. He hadn't been a dad—yet. Without a thought, he signed on for the "add water and insta-dad plan," while accepting my three kids and putting his own bun in my oven at the same time. I'm grateful and thankful for his acceptance of me and my kids while expanding our family at the same time. Friends for the prior thirty years, we were married in short order.

Jay was a civil engineer and had a great job he enjoyed. But then, the economy took another big dump and his salary was literally cut in half. My traction and success in network marketing was growing—but not enough to warrant these losses we were experiencing. Then, my company closed unexpectedly. Talk about a hit.

Two years later, with our home on the brink of foreclosure, having recently filed bankruptcy, with no money to invest in a new venture, and bills piling up, Jay and I weren't sure how we'd pull it off.

But, there was no question we would.

I was truly at a fork in the road.

There were two options before me:

1) Working for peanuts in the corporate world. I equated with this option akin to selling my soul and paying Uncle Sam first.
2)) Taking a risk with a brand-new network marketing company.

I talked with my husband about the options. While Jay knew I was passionate about the new opportunity and disheartened by the idea of returning to the corporate world, he was a bit reluctant…at first.

Thankfully, I didn't have to go back to my old ways of working hard at great personal cost and little reward. A serendipitous collision with a brand-new network marketing company gave me hope. My curiosity was piqued when I heard the name of the organization.

After researching the products and learning about their structure designed for collective success, I understood there was nothing like this company in the market.

I was so excited, the hairs on the back of my neck stood up as I considered a completely new trajectory for my family's life. Before I could start, we had to pull the money from somewhere for the $400 to invest in our new business. Needless to say, we pulled it together. We chose not to pay our house payment and invest in us instead.

I knew this could be a great situation. Jay's final vote of confidence before I leaped in, "Okay, but you better jump in with both feet and don't look back! Because you don't have a choice."

That's exactly what I did in August of 2014. It's also how my first "why" became to put my family first, and the second "why" to change other's lives was secured.

Thanks to our abundant success, a perk this team embraces, is a focus on local charities to pay the wealth forward and make a difference in our community.

Money may not buy happiness, but the ability to help others most certainly does. Ok wait, have you heard this before? I am calling BS. Money makes everything a hell of a lot easier.

In case you weren't sure, we are a husband and wife team that loves to help others with our whole heart. My youngest daughter is even better at this business than we are. She'll talk to **anybody** about the products that we market; if someone compliments her , she'll say, "You need to talk to my mom, right now." She posts on social media about it, and loves helping out the family. So, another great thing about network marketing is that you can totally pimp out your kids! LOL.

As I've mentioned, "Changing a person's life" is my secondary "why." I consider it an honor and privilege to walk alongside network marketing partners, as their whole life opens up through their work in network marketing. Following are five ways network marketing can change a person's life:

1. Network marketing empowers single moms to confidently generate sustainable income to support themselves and their children; while also creating the freedom to enjoy spending time with their children.
2. Network marketing enables spouses to partner and support one another in expanding financial wealth; while nourishing a greater personal connection.
3. Network marketing maximizes personal relationships and substantiates a significant return; while making connections and offering valuable products.
4. Network marketing instills confidence and breeds success; while greater and greater levels of influence and sales are achieved.
5. Network marketing engages and enlivens the community; while offering proceeds to "pay it forward."

Disclaimer-It takes time and more time in the beginning and you will have to sacrifice

Whether you have already launched your business, or if you're still in the whiteboard phase, know your "Why." It will help you stay committed to your dream and help bring others on board too. If you're unsure, visit www.tonivans.com/toolkit for a free checklist that will help you determine your why.

I encourage you to identify what one Big, Hairy Audacious Goal (BHAG) is—the one you want to reach more than anything else. Network marketing can help you get there, but you need a **Why**. It is a powerful motivator to help you get where you want to be.

You "Why" should pull on your heartstrings and be so strong it makes you cry.

My "Why" has changed since we first started. At first, I just wanted to pay my house payment and get it caught up. My chairman told me I wasn't dreaming big enough. His prod started my big journey, introduced me to a much bigger "Why," and a different BHAG—a house in a warm climate, on the water (more on that later)!

EFFING SIMPLE HOMEWORK

I'm a passionate female entrepreneur who works extremely hard to make my life more fulfilling and enjoyable. I take great pride in working for myself and I am motivated by empowering others to reach their true potential. You can determine or re-evaluate your "Why" by asking yourself these four questions. Your why will motivate you to get your ass out of bed:

Why do I want to move forward?

I want to be able to earn an income that helps our family. I want to continue being a SAHM & allow my husband to enjoy layoffs.

Why am I involved in this business, or why do I want to be involved in the business that I'm considering?

The products have changed my hair & confidence for the better. I also love the team I am apart of.

Do I love what I do? Why or why not?

Yes I do. Helping Woman gain confidence is an amazing feeling.

Do I have a passion for what I do? Why or why not?

I do, I just lost it for a bit.

What might be my driving "Why?"

My growing family. My husband Tal works so hard & I want to help him make our dreams come true.

We are drawn to leaders and organizations that are good at communicating what they believe. Their ability to make us feel like we belong, to make us feel special, safe and not alone is part of what gives them the ability to inspire us.

Simon Sinek

Chapter 2

Effing Simple Energy

The short version of this chapter is that you have to be completely resistant to the negatives. You have to kick negativity in the butt. You have to kick the word "no" to the curb. Happy people have bigger pay checks, and are in the hospital less often. True story that I'll talk about a little later on.

All you have to do is shift your mindset, but that's a lot harder than it sounds. You have to mind your mind. I start my day with positive energy, from the moment I wake up. Before I even get out of bed; grateful to be waking up another day, saying some of my mantras or devotions, and setting the tone for my day. <u>Miracle Morning</u>, by Hal Elrod is a must read book for your arsenal. Among other things he teaches, Elrod explains how you can get your day off to a magical start by setting your alarm an hour earlier than your usual wake-up time. From there, you focus on a positive intention, and creating a daily routine that shifts your perspective to the positive, no matter what's going on in your life.

To download my Daily 7 Success Starters to get your mornings off to a great start, visit www.soeffingsimple.com.

We have to mind our mind, and that's a battle in and of itself. We are subject to so much negativity in life. On average, we have tens of thousands of negative thoughts that float around in our brains, every day. Positive thoughts comprise 10-20% of our thinking, on average. Negative energy repels positive energy, so negative energy and thoughts repel success and happiness. You can either choose to be grateful for what you have, or lament what you don't have.

Money is energy. T. Harv Eker wrote a book that was life-changing me; Secrets of the Millionaire Mind. If you can understand money as energy, and energy as money, you'll see things in a different way. In fact, let me tell you a story that really defines what I'm talking about here. Money works in the Universe as energy, as something that is a good thing. If you can wrap your head around that, you will have conquered about 90% of the battle. Just the sheer belief in yourself is what will help you believe you can do it. But the one key thing people struggle with is self-confidence. This is why daily mantras are so important.

When I first met the owner of the current network marketing company we are working with, he immediately told me to start dreaming bigger. I wasn't dreaming big enough. I didn't have any BHAGs—yet. I had a very mediocre and worker-mentality mindset. Despite the fact that my very first check for the company was $8,900, I still didn't see the real potential. I knew we had something special going on, but I couldn't quite wrap my head around it. I did not have vision.

This owner asked me, "Toni, what is it that you want from this business?" Now, at the time, the previous company I worked with, and had great success with, closed down. I had not really worked or had a steady income for two years. We had gone through all of our savings, and were living on our credit cards. We were behind in our house payments, and I was on my third interview for some corporate job, paying $80,000 a year. In my gut, I knew this new company was either going to be the next global company of our generation, or it was going to suck.

As I was sitting there with the owner, thinking this through, I looked at him and said these nine words, "Dude, I just want to pay my house payment." He looked back at me, shook his head and says, "No, no, no, no...Your dreams have to be much bigger." So, I said to him, behind heavy emotions and flowing tears (ha I was bawling like a baby), "You know, the one thing that I've always wanted was to live someplace warm, by the ocean, so I would never, ever have to see snow again." He smiled softly back to me and said, "Ok, now we're getting somewhere!"

We continued to chat. Then he turned to me and said, "You know, if you stay with this for the next two or three years, and you work as hard as we've seen you do so far, you'll be earning seven figures a year." I just laughed, and said, "Yeah, whatever." He said, "Toni, I promise you—I have big dreams. If you stay with us for the next five to seven years, you'll be earning seven figures a month!" I just thought, "Whatever." Honestly, I thought he was full of it.

What he told me that day, instilled in me the belief that I could truly do what I wanted if I would only dream bigger. Guess where I live now—less than five short years later? Yup, on the ocean, in a warm part of the country where there's no snow, in a beautiful home. I pay cash for everything, have eradicated debt, and enjoy multiple investments and streams of income.

When we started with this new network marketing company, we took off like a rocket. By year two, we **were** bringing in seven figures. In the third year, the lid blew off. But, I still had money issues, namely guilt from making so much money. My mind hadn't caught up with the pay check we were earning. You have to have faith in you and your abilities—because you can! You have to reward yourself for making your goals, setting new ones, and reaching those. I still struggle with that, and work on it to this day.

People around us saw us differently and would say things like, "Look at you now, you're lucky, you have everything." I would tell them, "Bullshit, I'm not lucky! I work my ass off every single day." I work harder now than I ever have. But the "you have everything comment," it's mostly true.

Another "a-ha" moment I had was in Hawaii, when I was sitting with the CEO's wife, Carolina, who I've known since we started in the business. She had to bootstrap, from a really rough life, along with her husband and father-in-law, to become multi-millionaires from another network marketing company before starting their own.

Picture us in the cabana, drinking fruity drinks, in Maui on an all-expense paid incentive trip at the 5-star Grand Wailea, just chatting. I couldn't relax because something was on my mind. We were talking about the different challenges of the business, and I decided to share my concerns. I said, "You know, I don't know how to handle the money aspect of this business; I feel guilty. I don't know how to get my mind around it." She looked at me, and put it all in perspective. "Toni, how many years have you worked?" I told her, "All my life, since I was eleven years old." She paused, looked at me again, and said, "You've worked really hard. This is the fruit of your labor! This is what you have prepared yourself to do. Don't you think that's enough reward for your more than thirty years of working so hard? This is your reward for working so hard your whole life. You deserve this."

You and you alone must believe in yourself. If you believe that you can do what you set your mind to, you **will** succeed. But you can't allow your belief to waiver. There are people that believe in you, and there will be people who don't—and believe it, it is OK. It is a bit terrifying. However, once you commit to going into action, that fear dissipates or goes away once you get into things. You build belief and self-confidence over time. This is where your leader will lock arms with you and help you. We are your biggest cheerleaders and your success is paramount! We want nothing for you but effing simple success!

Please know this: the first time you step out in your belief...*you will want to puke.* Your will learn through trial and error...think about the last time you learned something new. The same thing happens the second and third time you step out. By the fourth time, you will feel a little better. The fifth time, you will be able to breathe without passing out. The sixth time you step out, your shortness of breath disappears. Essentially, the more you practice something new, by doing it again and again, it gets easier.

We aren't born experts at anything. Are some of us born with a special skill set? Yep, but most of us have to work continuously to get even close to being good at something. It takes seven years to become an expert at one thing—that's

10,000 hours! Because our society changes so rapidly, there's always something new to learn.

Seriously, what do you have to be afraid of? Does the word "No" scare you? Why do we give that one more word so much power? Whether it is a lifestyle choice, hobby or a business, you have the power to overcome the objection of "No" and be all that you can be.

"No" is just a word. It can mean any one of the following:

- I'm not interested right now, but I may be in the future.
- I'm not ready to make a commitment just yet.
- I need more information.
- I am not interested, but I might know someone that may be.
- And then there is the "**Eff No**, get away from me!"— Take those off your list.

Objections, or "Nos," are people calling out for more information. I have a handout that we use to train our team members on how to counter and answer, and offer information, when someone has an objection. You can download it at www.soeffingsimple.com.

Also, as my husband Jay likes to point out, being told "No" doesn't have to shake your confidence—especially when you are secure and the answer comes from a place of integrity. He notes, "I know I'm lovable no matter what—if I get a 'No,' it doesn't take away from who I am."

Combining telling the truth with integrity while saying "No" can be powerful. Jay notes, "I respect you enough to say no. It's not a no for you personally, nor is it a no for our relationship. It's a no on that issue, or it's a no for now." These are important distinctions not many people make. When this perspective is added to confidence and belief in yourself, it helps make you unshakable and unstoppable in your pursuit for success.

Life can throw curve balls, hard balls, even walks, and that damn ball can hit you straight between the eyes. Don't forget it can also give you a home run when the bases are loaded! Remember, we can circumvent many of these "wild" pitches. There is a two-book series called "The Happiness Advantage: How a Positive Brain Fuels Success in Work and Life" and "Before Happiness: The 5 Hidden Keys to Achieving Success, Spreading Happiness, and Sustaining Positive Change," where it is statistically proven that happy people are more successful. Author, Shawn Achor reported in Harvard Business Review:

Research shows that when people work with a positive mindset, performance on nearly every level— productivity, creativity, engagement—improves. Yet happiness is perhaps the most misunderstood driver of performance. For one, most people believe that success precedes happiness. "Once I get a promotion, I'll be happy," they think. Or, "Once I hit my sales target, I'll feel great." But because success is a moving target—as soon as you hit your target, you raise it again—the happiness that results from success is fleeting.

To achieve and sustain the success you desire, find your happiness first. Most of all, being happy often means finding a way to let all of the negativity and small, insignificant problems roll off your back. Doing this is a huge part of moving forward and not getting stuck or buying into the negative responses. My consistent mantra for dealing with rejection is, "Be a Ducky and let it roll off!" My husband pounded that phrase into my head on a daily basis for a long time. Shake your tail feathers! Sometimes you have to say "What the hell?" move forward, and don't look back. And if you have a naysayer it is just time to say *bye Felicia!*

Continually putting yourself out there when it comes to your business takes time, and hearing a lot of "Nos." If you're not getting at least 20 "Nos" every week, you're not putting yourself out there enough. Shit, make it 50!

Success may not happen overnight, next week, or even next year—you have to put in the time. With that said, as you approach others and work toward your goal, you will see things shift. Things always shift, whether you believe it or not. You get what you put in. The age-old word we hear about the effort you put out returning is "karma." While that's part of it, there's more.

If you are thinking negative and hurtful thoughts, that's what appears in your life. Your energy is very, very powerful. It can hurt you or help you. This is why it is so important to feed your mind with positive thoughts, books, programs, coaching, people, and more. According to Deepak Chopra, MD in "The Basics of Quantum Healing, "It's estimated that the average human has 60,000 thoughts a day. This is not surprising. What is disconcerting is that 90% of the thoughts you have today are the ones you had yesterday."

Your mind works to maintain and categorize all these thoughts. If you want to have different thoughts (and experience different results), it's important to seek, reveal, interact with, and nurture new thoughts instead of recycling the same ones. The biggest way I see people stay with the same, negative thought patterns is in what they consume.

They spend hours watching television, reality shows, and news. It may rock their world, but it's temporary, outside themselves, and is rarely beneficial. Most forms of media are one-sided outlets that drain you.

Are you ever around a person and feeling like their energy is draining you, or you just don't want to be around them? It's the field of energy they are radiating. On the opposite end of the spectrum, there are people whose presence you crave. These are people you want to be around all the time. They are always happy, always helpful, and you feel good simply by being around them. These are people coming from true graciousness. We need more of those people in our lives (and in this world).

"Attitude is gratitude." Do you wonder why that's a thing? It is one of the oldest cliché sayings in the world. But you know what? Wait for it…it is freaking true. Do you like being around the Eeyores of the world or the Tiggers?

Get on the bus—the bus of unlimited potential—and happiness awaits you. When you shift your thoughts and come from a place of gratitude, everything will shift in your life. Many are proof, I am proof. Period.

Are you willing to do what it takes? Most of you will not. Sorry, that's another fact. Most people will stay in mediocrity. If this pisses you off; it should. Mediocrity sucks! Congratulations. You may be one of those people that will actually get off their lazy ass and do something.

Nike said, "Just do it!" That's where potential begins and stagnation ends. Plain—effing simple.

Once you jump in, here's something else to consider. How much more would you be invested in your success if you were the owner of the business you work for? Would you work differently (harder, more frequently, or more efficiently)? What if you knew you could make a few extra hundred dollars in your first month, and upwards of $1,000 in your second month or more?

With network marketing, 12 to 18 months in, you could be looking at an extra $5,000 a month with amazing tax advantages. That's more than the household income of the average American family. According to the US Census Bureau, that's $57,617 a year, or $4,801 a month (2016 figures).[1]

What if I told you you could achieve this level of success by getting on the phone with two to three people a day, while spending one hour of your time having conversations that feel natural to you? If a person showed you a business model that leveraged the time of others, and helped you every step of the way, would it sound doable to you?

Not only is it doable, I've done it. I will teach you how to do it—and build your confidence along the way.

Don't be afraid of a little hard work to secure your future to live debt free. That's only the beginning of the extraordinary life you can lead. Not to mention, it's effing simple!

Looking back, taking the corporate job would have been the "responsible" move to make. Deep down, I knew it was best to give this network marketing business a shot, rather than regret not going for it. I had not been an "employee" in almost 20 years, and I was a serial entrepreneur.

Four years later, here I am. Our team consistently generates $25-35 million a month or more. Yes…you read this correctly! By the time this book is published, we'll be a billion dollar team.

Again, I am not a corporate gal. Working for peanuts with a set schedule is not for me. Now, I am able to travel with my family all the time. I know so many people in corporate positions and/or those who have a brick and mortar business. They frequently struggle to take time off when their children are sick, or they need to take personal time off. This often means paying outrageous day care fees, wondering what their children are up to all day, worrying about day care providers, working over-time, and dealing with other concerns, and using PTO.

I personally cannot stand being an employee. Some people need and want to be an employee—and if you are happy, then that is a great fit. But, the sad fact is that most people hate their jobs. I like to give orders (and freedom) much better than take them. Plus, I know that when there is an issue or mistake, there is only one person to blame—me.

Both of my parents had a strong work ethic, yet my dad's job ran his life. My old job used to run mine too. Not anymore. There's no question a structured work schedule would limit my income (not to mention the limits it would impose on my family life and travel schedule).

Thanks to the freedom our positions afford us, our daughter is home-schooled so she can travel with Jay and me. This business provides a vehicle for us to travel as a family. I am able to do so much more with my children than I ever could do before making network marketing my profession. People get stuck in a hamster wheel questioning how they will provide, when all they really need to do is decide to create change.

The best way to create change is to be open to the opportunities that present themselves and be coachable and keep learning.

EFFING SIMPLE HOMEWORK

What are the things, people and activities that make you happy?

Spending time w/ my family, taking the boys fishing & swimming

What are things, people and activities that give you energy?

Personal development, my team, thinking of the big dreams we have

What are things, people and activities that drain your energy?

People who are doing the same thing they were years ago w/ no dreams or goals

What kinds of shifts do you need to make to put happiness in front of your life?

Keep the negative people out of my life. Keep the big dreams & goals right in front of me.

I'm going to role model the energy I wish the world had.

Brendon Burchard

Chapter 3

Effing Simple Drama Ditch

Drama is so prevalent in life and in business—especially with woman, the topic of drama deserves its own address.

I am a reformed drama mama. For the most part, I let the drama mama in me go. Occasionally, I still participate in drama. However, when I do so now, I do it knowingly rather than being unknowingly swept up in it.

Don't get me wrong, everyone faces challenges. Sometimes the only thing we need to survive a challenge is a five-minute pity party so we can release it, learn from it, and move forward. Life is full of roller coaster twists and turns.

How we react to the ride and the inventible ups and downs, twists, turns, and stomach drops make all the difference.

There was a time when I let the roller coaster ride of life weigh me down. I was ridden with negativity. I was a champion at playing the victim role instead of trying to be a victor. I blamed my divorces, my problems, and my dwindling finances, on someone else instead of taking responsibility for them and taking charge of creating something different. Through these experiences, I learned that being negative and being a victim go hand in hand. Also, it was clear that this combination wasn't benefiting me and helping me create the success I desired.

When "The Secret" came out, I cannot tell you how many times I watched it—over and over and over again. The concepts presented in the movie (mainly the law of attraction) started me on my path to do things differently. As I watched and learned more, every day, my mindset and outlook got a little better and a little better. I was passionate about changing my life and my circumstances. Finally, I realized that no one but me could be the catalyst to the change I desired.

At the time, I had zero self-belief. Plus, no one was holding me accountable—especially not me.

I quickly realized I had to stop the patterns that kept me stuck. Part of that meant stepping away from negative relationships and people that were holding me back. I recognized I participated in nasty, toxic relationships. More importantly, I realized I was the captain of that ship.

Change comes with time and consistency in repeating positive actions. It rarely comes overnight or from one major overhaul. I recognized that this girl had lots of work to do! Little by little, I started turning off the news. Instead of reading fiction novels, I started reading self-development books. I turned to Steven Covey, W. Clement Stone, Hal Urban, and Louise Hay as authors to enrich my mind and path. I started reading just 10 minutes every day. I stayed committed—even though I was running two small businesses and starting network marketing on the side, I didn't really have time for anything. Yet, I wanted to be more than the poster child for busyness.

If you're reading this book, I know you can relate. I congratulate you on taking steps to do the self-work you need to succeed.

Through my self-work, I started to realize that my thoughts were just like food. You put garbage in, garbage comes out. Also, what comes out often smells like a sewer. I didn't want to keep knocking myself and others out with the sewage I spewed (much of it fueled by drama). I vowed to stop my addiction to drama, the people and, the media that kept me addicted to it.

I find that women are much more drama addicted than men. Sorry gals, it is the truth. Look at social media for one example. You know what I am talking about, so don't sit there and shake your head.

Let me ask who in your group does the following:

- Consistently talks about people behind their back (whether it is their child, spouse, or family member or friend)
- Always puts themselves down
- Considers the cup half empty instead of half full? (I call this the Eeyore complex, because on a beautiful, sunny day they will complain about rain).

One thing I learned after reading "A Complaint Free World" by Will Bowen is complaining and doing any of the above takes power away from you—every time you do it. Plus, when you are on the receiving end of complaint, even listening to someone complaint, you are participating.

Thus, you're giving away power.

Now, when this happens, (and I am far from perfect) I stop midsentence. I'm clear that I do not wish to be a part of something unless we are trying to help or solve a problem. Everything else is simply a complaint—half the time there is not even a point!

I no longer choose to give my energy and power away in ways that don't further my goals.

Jon Gordon, in his book, "Energy Bus," talks about energy vampires. These are people who suck the living life out of you with their negativity. What I have learned from coaching and helping others, from listening to them, is that they have got to bless and release people and situations that do not serve them. Those people and situations will drag you down the toilet. I have flushed close family, friends, and business associates, because. ain't nobody got time for that. Give yourself effing permission not to let these vampires suck the life out of you!

Drama is always going to drain energy you need. To build any business, you need a lot of energy. Any situation or person that is going to drain your energy, and your ability to build your business and life, is what you need to avoid, just like you would steer clear of a vampire. If you are following your path and passion, you never feel tired. And, part of that is being able to deflect and ditch negative energy and drama.

I can run circles around young adults. I was in my yoga class recently, surrounded by size two, skinny twenty-year-olds, and I was kicking their ass. When you are not on your path, however, whether you have a corporate job or your own business, it's exhausting. It will take every bit of energy out of you. However, it's not always easy to ditch the drama, is it?

Professionals don't do drama. They do business…they are beacons of positivity and light. And one last thing I want to share as I recently learned: gratitude and love have the highest vibration out there. Let's vibrate!

EFFING SIMPLE HOMEWORK

Go back to your "why?" statements. What's been holding you back? This can be situations, people, or anything that might be sucking your energy.

Not truly believing that I can do. it. My fear of what people may think of me.

How can you let go of the vampires, people or situations, that are keeping you in place?

Knowing that anyone that has anything to say has nothing to do w/ me.

What is your biggest lesson to learn when it comes to believing in yourself? This can be prior "a-ha" moments, or something that has come out of reading this book, so far.

I am capable of anything if I put my mind to it.

Persistence overshadows even talent as the most valuable
resource shaping the quality of life.

Tony Robbins

Chapter 4

Effing Simple Thirst

If you don't want your own version of success, and I mean really want it more than anything else; as much as you want to breathe, as much as you want to live, you have not developed a thirst that will propel you to your success. Again, that your "Why" has to make you cry. Being coachable sets you up for success.

While the alliance with my current network marketing organization feels complete, finding my true fit did not come easily.

My first attempts at network marketing were met with frustration because I wasn't committed to me, the organization, or the work required to create the personal success and team success I desired. Looking back, it's clear what was in the way of fulfilling my dreams.

I noticed the way I approached business came from a self-centered place with too much ego on board. Everything was about me—always and in all ways.

Hard-headed and determined, I came face-to-face with a money block that stemmed from childhood—I grew up believing making money was for assholes.

It's no wonder I didn't make the money I desired. I most definitely am not that type. Nor is money only for assholes.

Once I realized this childhood belief was holding me back, I approached business in a different way.

Gifted with the lessons I learned from network marketing, I moved forward. Network marketing was starting to blossom as a personal and professional development program in disguise. I was dedicated to being coachable and improving my mindset. I knew I hadn't been partnered with the right companies at the right time. You could say my mind and heart were not aligned with the companies I partnered with. To realign, I decided to stop marketing and putting energy into businesses and ideas that did not match who I was as a person and the skills I had to offer.

In other words, I'd had enough of my own bullshit and decided to make a change.

However, the incongruity between the money I desired and the block around money being associated with assholes held me back.

There's no doubt the stakes were high when I joined a new start-up network marketing company. I didn't let that stop me. Instead, I decided to jump in with both feet and relinquish my long-held money block.

The only looking back was to cultivate and apply the experience and lessons I accumulated working in the network marketing industry during the prior two decades. In three years' time, my track record for generating success, coupled with my network marketing experience, catapulted me into becoming a top producer in organizational sales and income. As if that wasn't enough, I was the first representative to reach the Million Dollar Club with a new network marketing start-up—in two short years. (I was recently recognized in their Five Million Dollar Club.)

I knew at a young age my work ethic was strong. Truth be told, I was fascinated by the network marketing industry for a very long time. I had some successes and some failures— *huge ones*—on both sides. However, I knew network marketing was my path. I tell you, I'm sure glad I listened to my gut on that one. It is not often that we listen to ourselves, but your intuition is the holy grail of "You have to do it!" It's Divinity guiding you to the great purpose you're meant to pursue. While intuition is something many of us have been taught to ignore, I've found it to be a key factor in my continued success.

Using our intuition is only one part of the success equation though. I've found we must also have a great thirst for success as well—and success has a different meaning for each individual. Most of us inherently inhabit that thirst. However, if we are not coachable, the thirst is not one that's quenched. It's sad to see the potential outcome that someone can experience in their lives—if only they were coachable enough to let go of what they think should happen in order to create that success—and, go after that success with passion.

Can you be successful without being coachable? The short answer is no and no.

Every day, in my workshops and in my coaching practice, I experience individuals with great thirst who fail to perform and produce in a way that generates success. I frequently run into those who miss out on greatness because they resist an exercise or assignment. It often shows up as individuals being offended by the way I do (or do not do) certain things. They forget why they signed up in the first place, and get caught in the trap of their own thinking.

As a coach and mentor, I love to help people reach a goal and attain financial freedom from a deep desire to succeed. However, that success comes more easily, quickly, and profoundly when recruits are coachable.

Here are the activities someone with a coachable spirit engages in:

- Regularly asking for help, instruction, guidance, and advice—while being receptive to the advice as given.
- Taking notes, reading books, and learning from others who are experiencing the kind of success they wish to achieve.
- Asking questions—even when it may reveal their ignorance and risk looking or feeling stupid.
- Listening to others carefully and patiently with a desire to learn.
- Attempting new things, even when they don't feel experienced or competent at that thing.
- Accepting responsibility for things that don't go as planned, failures, and flops, rather than blaming anyone and everyone else.
- Seeking one-on-one personal guidance and mentoring. And, investing in further coaching when ready to advance to new levels. But, be wary. Those who say they can teach it, but they can't do it, are full of shit. Only accept coaching from those who are much more successful than you are and make more money than you do.
- Seizing opportunities to learn from anyone and everyone—including others who have different views, come from different backgrounds, and those who are at different levels (behind and ahead in terms of perceived success).

- Moving through resistance to progress beyond personal comfort zones.
- Consistently reading, listening to, and being open to learning things that challenge their current beliefs.

Being coachable also includes the following attributes:

- Awareness of personal knowledge and abilities and the assertiveness to use them to their advantage.
- Acceptance of individual limitations, inabilities, and inexperience while actively seeking out others who can help teach them or take responsibility for them—delegation and trust in others are essential for success.
- Processing criticism and correction from a neutral place without becoming defensive, holding resentment or retaliating toward the person providing feedback.
- Capability to leave their zone of comfort and doesn't fear making mistakes.
- When failure occurs (as it inevitably will), coachable people persist. They seek help, try different things, and persist until they meet or exceed their mark.
- Flexibility to change their views and practices when convincing evidence is presented—even if it means admitting they are wrong.
- Willingness to surrender control coupled with faith in the process.

An inability to be coachable comes from a place of insecurity, fear, and low self-esteem. Being coachable on the other hand breeds confidence.

Many people get stuck when success doesn't come easily. We're conditioned to focus on the negative, but that will never move us forward in a sustainable way. A success story that comes to mind is a leader I refer to as "The Comeback Kid." She's a younger woman still cultivating her leadership skills. After growing to a very high network marketing rank, her business went completely backwards—all the way to the bottom of the hierarchy. She would cry, get upset, and be negative. She went almost a year not being paid her career title.

I always ask my down-line if they want me to sugar coat my feedback, or give it to them straight. Most opt for the latter. It makes it much easier, when they are coachable and self-motivated. In this case, I told The Comeback Kid to "Stop your whining and get back on that horse! Build a new team!"

Thankfully, she listened and changed her approach. All of a sudden, I would see her numbers sneak up. She stayed the course and is now heading up a large downline and achieving her sales goals.

Having a coachable spirit will take you places that raw talent alone never could.

Another leader is "The Little Engine That Could." After a long period of growth and success, some like to fall back into management mode. However, with network marketing, a large percentage of your business is sales. You must continue to grow the team and find new people to add to your downline. Your personal business is key. You must be out meeting people and prospecting all the time. This is your #1 activity...read that again...#1!

I attribute my success to being coachable, accepting input from my mentors and team, and continuously looking for ways to improve my game. I'm rewarded for my coachable spirit through a hefty pay check and the ability to coach others to earn the same. When someone is interviewing with me, to join our organization, I try to nail down four things...

1) What is the person's "Why?"
2) What is their Big Hairy Audacious Goal (BHAG)?
3) Will they dedicate the time to match their income and vice versa?
4) How do they want me to hold them accountable, if they're not measuring up to what they told me they wanted?

During that conversation, I can find out if they're coachable. If they're not, I don't take them on.

Are you coachable?

EFFING SIMPLE HOMEWORK

In what ways do you consider yourself coachable? Explain.

_____

_____

_____

_____

In what ways do you think you might be difficult to coach?
Explain.

_____

_____

_____

_____

When is a time that you've coached someone, and been
frustrated by their lack of responsiveness? What could you
have done differently to have been more effective as a coach?

_____

_____

_____

_____

Name a specific time when you were not coachable. What happened? What would you do differently?

_____

_____

_____

_____

Just as we get well in community, our businesses succeed in partnership with one another.

Melissa Drake

Chapter 5

Effing Simple Partnerships

Have you heard the quote, "It is always better when we are together?" This phrase is true in network marketing and every home-based business. There's no way I could achieve the level of success I've enjoyed without the support and teamwork that Jay and I implement together and enjoy with our girls, Naomi and Catherine and especially to our amazing team (aka family). We experience success because of the support and teamwork we've cultivated as partners, as a family, and as a business. We also have a small number of employees that enable us to do what we do.

We are truly fortunate.

Some of the best teams in network marketing are husbands, wives, and families. As a couple, spouses can run a successful home-based business by sharing the workload while building, running, and recruiting for their business. As partners sharing a home, they divide the chores based on what needs to be done and who has the capacity to do them—regardless of outdated gender norms that dictate certain genders complete certain chores (except nursing and giving birth). As business partners, spouses keep each other focused on the business aspirations, help manage one another's time, and motivate each other. They can set goals together, and brainstorm ways to grow their business. Bringing up children in this industry also brings in a hugely different dichotomy as well.

Not sure how to bring your spouse or family on board? Here's how:

If your significant other isn't already in network marketing, get them involved, get them to a meeting and give them a plan upfront. This doesn't have to mean joining the business, it's simply a matter of support. Spouses ask us all the time, "How can I help?" Our advice is always the same. It begins with a suggestion to help the business any way you can—whether that's making calls, sending emails, delivering samples, or staying on top the bookkeeping tasks, before they become unmanageable. When you have children, there are always ways to help with their care. Don't forget about all the tasks that go into managing your home as well.

Become a strong partner behind the scenes and on the front lines of your home and business. In doing so, you will strengthen your business (and your partnership). Two productive people in a business have always been stronger than one. Two connected people in a relationship motivate one another while the connection deepens.

I actually like Jay much more now—than I did five years ago. Today, we are a force. We are united. We are a power couple. But it wasn't always that way. In the beginning, he poo-pooed everything about network marketing. He said only a few make big money. He believed the few that were successful preyed on their family and friends, and that only a few were lucky…

WRONG, WRONG, WRONG! Now he's gone from a naysayer, to supporting me, to loving our products, and to be an integral part of our presence. But for the men becoming a part of this, it has to be their idea. Today, Jay is an icon. He wears his status well. Plus, he's so proud of what we can do for others through network marketing, noting "I am a pathway to salvation."

He means that in the best way—and backs it up daily. He holds the standard as a spouse and business partner. He holds people accountable, and he calls people on their bullshit. Plus, that man keeps me in check—which may be the hardest part of his job (and the only part that's not effing simple).

I don't claim to be easy.

I tend to fly off the handle and be overly emotional. In fact, still to this day, I'm guilty of getting caught up in drama on occasion. He is my sounding board, my love who reminds me "Hey, you are being crazy and need to get your shit in check."

Basically, he is the one that brings reason in a direct way. You can't skirt around issues with him. Jay keeps me grounded; through wins and losses.

Sugar coating doesn't exist for either of us—and it shouldn't for you. Jay is brutally honest…and that serves me, him, and our team.

Imagine the power that honesty, direction and stability can bring to your team in a growing network marketing company. Then multiply it by two and that's what Jay and I offer—except, when we combine our power it's not multiplied, it's magnified tenfold

Go for it! Your time is now. You can do it! We are proud of everyone who chooses to launch and manage a network marketing business. Whether you do it solo or as part of a partnership, you are amazing!

When Jay was working as an engineer, I told him he was costing us money by working. I suggested it was time to retire. He didn't think twice. He jumped in at first at the opportunity to start being a stay at home dad. He makes a better mom than I do. Now we are doing better than ever and he eventually started doing the business with me and we are doing better than ever. Even with his great job as a civil engineer, our combined education, and my network marketing business, we still struggled.

This doesn't mean Jay's transition to network marketing was easy. As many men do, I could see the way Jay tied his identity to his work. When that was no longer his reality, he underwent a huge adjustment period. At the time he made the switch, I was making more money than I ever had. My income was four times what Jay was bringing home. I wanted to travel more, and I really wanted Jay to be home with and for the kids. After five or six months of managing our home and taking care of the kids, he blossomed into the role of the leader at home and manager of the business details. And, he was a pro at handling the kids.

Today, I often joke that Jay makes a better mother than I do. I am more of a doer, and I am the person that always wants to go places. We complement each other really well as parents. Jay is strong where I am not, and vice versa. He has so much more patience with effing simple homework. He's more likely to get on the floor and play—I just do not have patience for that.

A few years ago, Jay became more involved with the business and noted the opportunity to bring more men into network marketing. He was onto something! We paired up and started doing network marketing as a family business. We travel together all the time and we and are a lot closer.

Although our network marketing company has dedicated men's products, our team was missing the boat on getting the men involved. Jay and I saw a huge opportunity and really started to impress upon the company, and the public, that network marketing is an equal opportunity business. Jay was the token male for two full years before more and more couples, men, brothers, and dads got into the business.

We are both public speakers, and have similar, savvy strengths. However, our experiences—some of which are tied to our respective genders—enable us to bring different things to the table. We also play off each other's humor very well. It doesn't hurt that we can be blunt with each other.

According to the Direct Sales Association stats in 2017, 73.5% of network marketing entrepreneurs are women, even though it shouldn't be.[1] When a woman starts this type of business, a lot of time she doesn't have the support of her spouse. That brings an extra challenge to starting and succeeding in this type of business. If you are reading this, and this is your circumstance, you're really going to have to work even harder. Frankly, if you need your partner's "permission," that's bullshit. If you really, really want to do something positive for your family, your spouse should support you—period.

I believe one of the barriers to this support is, women often aren't transparent with their significant others. They don't sit down and say, "Hey, I found something I really want to do. It's going to take some work. It's going to take some time away. But, I know it's going to make a difference, and most importantly, it's something I need for my happiness." They need to sit down and have that conversation with their partner, their family, and kids who are old enough to understand it. This effing simple conversation will go a long way in helping them be on board with your new endeavor and potentially joining you on the journey. No matter what, you don't want your family to be resentful of the extra time it takes to launch and grow your business. Having this conversation up front helps lay the groundwork and expectation.

Ideally, the whole family is working together for success by keeping negativity out of the fold, and focusing on the positive. Your family can be a fortress to protect you from the shit outside. Some of us aren't lucky enough to have an existing family like this. That's ok. Jump in and go it alone to start, and build your family the way it was intended to be—full of support, love, and accountability for you to be your best self.

When you create positivity and a sense of success into your own life, maybe just maybe, it will be contagious to the rest of your family. The most important thing to remember is to persevere, no matter what! Many times, you can become the influencer in the family, and bring a shift in the energy of your business.

If your family isn't on board, it will be more challenging for you. At the same time, those you connect with through network marketing are the best family members you'll ever encounter. This includes your upline, downline, customers, and others in the industry. People in network marketing companies are motivated and focused on a common purpose focused on serving others.

Here is what Jay has to say about couples partnering in business: What doesn't make any sense to me, and never will, is when men come up to me and ask "How can I support my wife in business?" I'm not sure they've thought this question through, because it's really effing simple. Sometimes it feels like the guy is trying to get attention, and get credit for doing things he should automatically be doing as part of a partnership.

I remind husbands that supporting their wives in business is no different than supporting her at home. It's as simple as doing the following:

- Helping with the kids (school runs, doctor's appointments, effing simple homework help, play dates, and other things we do as fathers).
- Helping around the house (cleaning, organizing, doing the laundry, running errands, managing

sitters and housekeepers, taking care of the lawn, and other things we do as husbands).

To treat "business" differently is crazy. I often tell men, "Hey, guess what I did? I mailed *her* mail today. I mailed *her* mail, not *our* mail."

People get in their own way—men especially. The vast majority of the men I know have not plugged into how amazing this business can be. If they would stop and get involved in learning about the compensation plan, the products, and the business side, they would be farther along.

Instead, they approach network marketing as "My wife has a hobby." I guess it is because we are still trapped in the mentality that if our wives are not barefoot and pregnant, then we are going to lose them.

When I hear "Hey, how can I support her?" I believe it's the most ridiculous question ever.

These men do not understand.

The easiest thing for anyone to do is just ask their partner how their day is. It's more than asking though. It's important to actually care about how their day is, not to placate them, but to know how their day is. Toni and I talk about others' success, how the business is going, and potential problems or things that might come up. Toni and I never ask each other how our days are without really caring to hear the answer—good or bad. Caring helps us create and cultivate connection. When my 11-year-old asks how your day is, you better give her an answer because she really wants to know. She wants that connection too. If she can get it, why can't a 40 or 50-year-old man get it?

I have my mom to thank for that connection. Even though I had two parents, like most kids of the 70's, I was raised by my mom. My mom owned a hair salon near my grandma. I spent a lot of time at the salon with my mom and the women she served. Early on, I plugged into the fact that women are smarter than men. The sad truth is, women know this, but are scared to admit it! Instead, they were raised to take care of their men. Women feel this biological need to uplift their husband—when in fact, the elevation needs to work both ways.

When the network marketing opportunity came along, neither Toni or I realized how big it would become. However, we both knew if the products performed as they claimed, I had no doubt Toni would be successful. It was a ground floor opportunity—truly one of a kind.

I have no idea why men get upset when their wives are incredibly successful, make substantial amounts of money, and/or can retire their husbands. Why is this an issue and why do things fall apart?

I believe the root issue is fear. Men fear they will lose their manhood or their wives to the success, instead of realizing this is a business—one they can grow and enjoy *together*. It's a business that creates opportunity and further connection. Fear is represented in the stories we make up. Instead of fearing the success, we can choose to enjoy it instead!

Let's start with this: we made substantial amounts of money, and together, we decided to retire me. We actually put me to work doing something much harder than going to an office every day—supporting my wife and her growing business. Me being retired created an opportunity for me to support Toni. I'm able to manage what she needs most and in a way that's most beneficial for our entire family—myself included.

What man doesn't want that?

Me showing support to this business demonstrates to other men that Toni and network marketing businesses are credible. When a man supports a woman in network marketing, other men follow along.

In order to talk about how Toni and I work together, we must put some context in place. Toni and I have known each other since high school—that's more than three decades! We were best friends "back in the day." Even though we crossed paths a few times, we didn't start talking again until 2006. At that time, we both ended relationships. When we got together, our friendship picked up where we left it in high school.

I knew Toni had tried different network marketing avenues, but she was unemployed when we reconnected. She didn't know what she wanted to do when she moved to

Chicago. On the other hand, I had a great job, a good salary, per diem expenses, and a company car. I was making around $150,000 a year. It was a great job for a single guy, but perhaps not so great for a family. When Toni and I decided to move-in together, we were not aware that she was pregnant.

That was a beautiful surprise and blessing! I was 40 years old when Toni gave birth to our miracle child, Catharine in 2007. In 2018, I was honored to adopt Toni's older daughter, Naomi. Our family is now complete.

EFFING SIMPLE HOMEWORK

Do you feel that you have the support of your friends and family members in your network marketing efforts?

_____

_____

_____

_____

If you are single, or don't have the support of your spouse/significant other, what steps can you take to make sure you don't burn out? Is there a friend or family member you can enlist to help?

_____

_____

_____

_____

If you partner is resistant to network marketing, what steps will you take to protect your momentum in your network marketing business?

_____

_____

_____

_____

You were put on this earth to achieve your greatest self,
to live out your purpose, and to do it courageously.

Steve Maraboli

Chapter 6

Effing Simple Re-purpose

Before we decided to retire Jay, to help me in my business, things were getting difficult with our financial picture. When we first started living together, we had rented a few nice places, but Jay lost some money when he sold his "bachelor pad." We thought everything was solid for our family. Frankly, it was—for several years. We finally bought a nice house, but soon after, the economy tanked.

At the time, Jay was a civil engineer; federal funding dried up on all the projects he was working on. Thus, his income dried up and even though he kept his job, he was earning $25,000 less a year. We were very thankful that he still had a job, but we were overextended on the house.

Things became a little dicey; Chicago is a very expensive place to live, and a family of five does not work on a single-earner's income.

During this time, I heard about a new network marketing opportunity. We were behind four house payments and were working on a house payment modification. Before the start-up network marketing company came along, I already tried a few networking companies. I was making decent money with one of my businesses, but because of the economy, we were always playing catch-up.

Sketchy finances can—and do—break up couples. Jay and I had a firm foundation and we were always able to talk about things—including the uncomfortable things like our dwindling income, increased expenses, and the bills that piled up. Knowing each other for 33 years was a gift! We both knew we were hard workers, and if we found the right positions or opportunities, we'd be successful.

I had the opportunity to take a corporate job, but Jay was extremely leery. We both knew I would be more successful when the right networking company came along. We know success isn't always a product of just trying hard or working hard. There is something to be said for being open to "luck" and certain opportunities that present themselves to you.

Jumping on the new start-up was a no-brainer when it came about. I could be on the ground floor and put my skills to use to drive us forward. I jumped in, full speed ahead, and things certainly paid off, literally. My first check was $8,900! That was a lot for a month's worth of work.

We used that check to pay the mortgage and tried get caught up. That first big check gave us both the feeling of success. At the time, Jay was working on a big project, but his company's part in the deal was ending in 2015. His position was extended for another three months to finish up, and the economy was picking back up. Jay was getting more projects as a project manager, so things were looking up, finally.

The timing was interesting as the network marketing company took off and I needed to travel more. Even with Jay's raise and all the perks of a corporate job like benefits, we could not justify him working any longer. We needed a nanny to take care of the kids. At the time, I was making three to four times the amount Jay earned. We had a choice to make— have Jay stay in his job, or stay at home with the kids. While my business was building momentum, Jay was starting tire of being an engineer. He dreaded the doom of Sunday nights when Monday morning loomed.

Deciding to stay home was an easy choice, but not necessarily an easy transition. Jay is an older dad. Our daughter, Catherine was born when he was 39. She was seven years old when we changed things up. We both saw this as Jay's opportunity to stay at home with her while also taking care of our home and supporting my new business. His availability was a gift. It did not occur to him that he was retiring. He called it being "repurposed."

It does not feel like retirement. Frankly, he works just as hard on the business and our home life as he did at the office, if not more. It was a big adjustment for him.

While the transition was a big one, and it was outside of our comfort zone, there was nothing scary about it. We trusted each other, and we trusted the new business. When I saw what the company was doing and how fast it had grown, it made leaving his job much easier. There have been weird moments when people ask him what he does—only because what he does is somewhat "revolutionary" in today's world. As I mentioned earlier, not many men understand that not only is it ok to let a woman lead and be the main breadwinner, it's downright innovative and mutually rewarding. It's effing awesome!

Working through network marketing can be a challenge for those in the corporate world, or those with a 9-5. Even if they are an entrepreneur, and already have a business, exploring network marketing can work it is an insurance policy. I often ask these individuals, "Hey, what would happen to your brick-and-mortar business if you lost your arm tomorrow, or if something happened to you and you couldn't work there, anymore? Or god forbid something worse. What would happen to your finances? Could your family survive?"

With a successful network marketing business, you have residual income, where you don't necessarily have to do anything to make money. This is especially true once you've built up your network, and nurtured the relationships in your network marketing organization. In this way, sometimes the person being "repurposed" is you; you have to switch your way of thinking.

If you are in the corporate or 9-5 world, your mindset has to shift because network marketing is definitely not a Monday thru Friday, 9-5 job. If you're an entrepreneur, with a brick-and-mortar store, your focus needs to shift to emphasize relationships, and not so much store or office hours. Face to face communication is really important when network marketing. That is your bottom-line, number one! Social media, online presence, phone calls, emails, text messages; these are tertiary and only really good for getting you that face to face appointment. Successful entrepreneurs spread passion, cultivate passion, and relate to passionate people.

Changing from having an "employee mentality" is very difficult in our country. Entrepreneurs must be accountable. There are some people who are happiest punching a clock, being told where to be, and what to do every minute of the workday. And that's ok. But, I think some of us have been brainwashed to think that is what we are supposed to do and be. That's simply not true. Network marketing can be a ticket out of this type of mentality, and a way for you to repurpose yourself.

If this means that, while you transition from this world to the freedom that network marketing offers, you might have to calendar in time for yourself to work on your new business. I teach people that you can do this business no matter where you are. If you are in a hotel, for example, you can be talking to the hotel staff. You can talk to people in the airport. If you're in a restaurant, you damn well better be talking to that waiter, waitress, or bartender. Strike up casual conversations to talk about your business. This is a big shift from what we're used to in the corporate or 9-5 world. Service professionals, retail workers, teachers, and nurses make awesome business partners.

You can't expect to talk someone up or send spammy messages and think you will recruit them right there and then. That's the wrong mentality. Those actions are what gives network marketing its shady reputation. In terms of relationships, that's like trying to get a proposal on the first date! Before you propose, you have to spend time appreciating one another, understanding each other's needs, and working things out. There's a lot of massaging that takes place before "sealing the deal." People will do business with you when they know, like you, and trust you. You will hear this time and time again because it is true. This can take weeks, months and even years. This takes time and most importantly,

81

trust in the process. In many ways, you have to repurpose how you approach business and wrap your head around the steps it takes to gain momentum and close sales.

I've had people I have personally known for more than years before they finally said, "Yes!" They jumped in, worked the business like they needed to, and watched their income increase 2-fold, 5-fold, 10-fold. They were able to do this, because of one simple thing: belief. I work with people who believe in the business, their abilities and most especially, they are resilient. They succeed because they successfully repurposed themselves.

"A rising tide, floats all ships," says Stuart MacMillian. Be the rising tide for yourself, your family, your friends, and your network marketing organization.

EFFING SIMPLE HOMEWORK

What part of your life do you need to "repurpose?"

_____

_____

_____

_____

What are some challenges to repurposing for you as an individual, and if you have a family, for them as well?

_____

_____

_____

_____

If you know someone who is successful in network marketing, meet with them to find out how they repurposed themselves. What did you learn from them?

_____

_____

_____

_____

Because there's nothing more beautiful than the way the ocean
refuses to stop kissing the shoreline,
no matter how many times it's sent away.

Sarah Kay

Chapter 7

Effing Simple Environment

In the Spring of 2015, we started to have serious discussions about where we wanted to live and whether or not we should relocate. Jay had been in Chicago for a long time, and money was no longer an issue. This—coupled with technology, social media, and the ability to travel—meant we could live anywhere. Making a move is a big decision and we didn't want to make a mistake. It was scary.

We went to Charleston, SC, on vacation and quickly decided we wanted to live there. The first six months of Jay's retirement allowed me more time to travel. By this time, I felt I had destiny by the cajones. Jay shares with me how he found it so amazing to see me—as someone he loves— having so much fun, doing work that I loved.

Our professional success improved our relationship. The business elevated us and allowed us to do more with the kids. Within the first year with our current network marketing company, I was able to meet a BHAG—one I never before considered until I was challenged to dream bigger!

Having an effective environment to flourish in isn't just about locating yourself in the perfect city or neighborhood. Let's dial it back to the simplest of aspects. For example, do you have a working environment in your home where you feel comfortable and productive? Do you have a nice chair, desk, and a view? Most importantly, do you feel refreshed when you go into your workspace?

In the bigger picture, what type of community do you want to live in? Is it where you're currently located? Great! But, don't forget to dream BHAGs! Consider where would you want to live if money were no object. I'm proof that moving to a dream location can be your reality—if you want it and work hard enough. Go back to your roots, and influences, to tap into where you really, really want to be.

One word of caution: wait to get in your dream location after you start producing or radically change your life I always recommend you start in your own big backyard. That's a huge opportunity that many people miss. Your personal network, your significant other's network, heck—even your kids' networks, are where you start. From there, you can grow within your current community, and build a large enough network where you don't have to worry so much about your immediate location. Plus, thanks to technology and social media, your immediate location connects you to the world.

Environment isn't just about your physical space. It also includes your mental and emotional state. Are you creating a space of trust in yourself? Are you nurturing an emotional space where you can be liked and trusted? What kind of emotional and spiritual environment are you creating for yourself and your family?

A mistake I see people make all the time is they only join network marketing for the money. This is why most people start, and that is ok—most very quickly get the bigger picture. When money is the motivation, they're destined to fail. To realize the full potential of network marketing, you must come from a place of servant leadership with a servant's heart. You have to put the other person first and help them fulfil their greatest potential, whether that's finding the right products, helping them build their business, or training them to recruit others. Only then can you reach your greatest potential.

Most people think with their ego and come from a place of "What can you, or network marketing, do for me?" No, no, no, no, the whole "me," "my," "I" language doesn't work. The proper words are "we" and "ours." It's so much better to focus on creating a personal environment where you think, more often than not, "What can I do for you?" or "How can I serve you?" When you do this, you transform others and they become loyal to you.

Not only will this bring you joy, and a peace of mind, it will serve you well in your career. This has been my experience over many years of working in this world, and seeing it throughout our network marketing organization. I'm not special in any way when it comes to this. I see people, every day, in our downline doing this same thing, and truly transforming their own live and the lives of others.

In network marketing, this philosophy serving others is magnified. You are working for your team and supporting your team. Instead of thinking of what your team can do for you, you have to, daily, think of what you can do for your team. If you describe your network marketing business using, "I" versus "we" or "ours," you're doomed. The atmosphere you create has to be conducive to developing a true team environment. It's not even your team. Nope. It's **our** team!

If you create this type of culture, every person on the team can succeed—truly. I root for everyone in the network marketing structure to succeed. When we all succeed, we all succeed! That's the unique aspect of network marketing. When I see people, who are competitive with other members in their organization, I know it's a matter of time before things will implode on them. And it will be their own damn fault! Comparison is the thief of success and joy. Don't marginalize your success. Every customer and every new team member is a cause for celebration that gets you one step closer to your dreams. You have a different path and journey. Experience and embrace all of it. The ups the downs, the tears and the laughs, they all matter!

Building and a creating a positive culture and environment starts and ends with caring. In our current network marketing organization, I saw this from the owners. They do business with absolute sincerity, and a commitment to doing the right thing, while being 100% transparent and ethical.

You can't drag your team over the finish line, but you can cheer them on and help them along the way. it begins with modeling the right behavior and practicing what you preach. Everyone makes mistakes, and, when you are the leader of a network marketing team, you have to be able to coach, and demonstrate what it looks like to be coachable!

When things don't go as planned, and you need to direct someone differently, you can do so with love. I call this corrective action the Oreo Cookie Technique. Whenever I have to address a crucial situation with somebody, I first talk about something that is fantastic, and praise them. Even though I know everybody loves the middle, fluffy part of the Oreo cookie, that is the issue that you need to address.

From a coaching perspective, I want to ask them questions, like:

- What do you think we could do differently?
- What can we do so we don't have to address this again?
- What lessons can we learn from this type of experience?
- How can I support you?

The coaching is the learning part of the process. From there, you end on another good-note, the other crunchy, yummy part of the Oreo cookie. You end with praise, again. If they have that light bulb, or "a-ha" moment, then you know they will move forward in the right way; they now have more tools in their toolbox. If they ever come up with a similar situation, they now know how to handle it. And, you've helped create a productive, constructive, loving and support environment for the team.

Sometimes, the best strategy is to just shut up and listen. Wait for the other person to finish their sentence before you jump in. Create an environment where people feel like they can be heard and listened to.

In other words, create for others an environment and culture where everyone is likely to thrive. Create an environment and culture that you would like to work in. When you do that, you'll see your own personal power grow, and you'll see the team succeed to their incredible, and fullest potential.

EFFING SIMPLE HOMEWORK

Look honestly at your current environment, and in one-sentence, describe it below:

Physical:

Emotional:

Spiritual:

What changes do you need to make in each realm of your environment?

Physical:

Emotional:

Spiritual:

It isn't just what you know,
and it isn't just who you know.
It's actually who you know, who knows you,
and what you do for a living.

Bob Burg

Chapter 8

Effing Simple Onboarding or Recruitment Process

Recruiting and keeping a network marketing team together is not unlike forming a strong army—an army dedicated to a single cause and purpose. Without strong organization, clear communication flow, and strong leadership, the army will flail—and fail.

In our organization, we have a detailed checklist detailing where everyone ranks; what they're working on, and where they are headed. In this chapter, I'm going to outline the system I've developed to recruit team members, and nurture those relationships so everyone on the team, and in the organization, benefits. When you get your system down, you can onboard someone successfully in less than a half hour.

The things you need to consider, as you develop your system, are six components of an effective recruiting and onboarding process. The basic steps are as follows:

1. Get into the prospect's **"why."**
2. Discuss the **time** commitment.
3. Go through **income** potential.
4. Develop an effective **contact list.**
5. Cover **Income Producing Activities** (IPAs).
6. **Rinse and repeat (follow up)**—every single day.

Effective onboarding will save you, and your prospects, time. As you develop your system, and practice it over and over, and over again, you'll be able to tell when people are truly ready to jump in and be part of the team. If they aren't ready, be up-front and let them know two things.

1.) That's ok. You'd rather not waste their time or yours
2.) Ask them to call you when and if they're ready. I don't chase down prospects who aren't ready. I've found that to be a real waste of energy. Ain't nobody got time for that!

A person's why will give you a glimpse into their motivation and tell you whether they are dreaming big or not. Their availability and commitment to the time outlay for their desired income, indicates how dedicated they will be to putting in the work necessary to earn what they desire.

You can usually tell, once your prospect has gone through the exploration of their why, the time commitment, and the income structure, whether or not they're really ready. When they **indicate** they are ready by their actions and responses—not just because they say they are—but clearly, they are geared up to get things started; you can then begin to help them develop their contact list, and continue from there. It's effing simple!

Once they sign on, have them create a contact list by compiling contacts from their phone, email, social media (Facebook, Instagram, Twitter, LinkedIn), and other connections.

This is where they recall all the "FRANKS" in their life:

Friends
Relatives
Acquaintances
Neighbors
Kids
Social Media/Social Circles

Don't stop there…Have them think about the groups and clubs they belong to, the activities they enjoy, and the people they interact with. Consider things like knitting clubs, book clubs, church groups, sporting events, and retail encounters.

You should do this exercise and you ask everyone on your team to do the same thing. There is no reason you can't come up with 500 to 1000 names on your list. Doing this exercise alone, and then contacting each person, can make a huge difference between success and failure.

Your contact list equals your pay check. A larger contact list equals a larger pay check. This list should be a living and breathing document you add to everyday. A digital document is a perfect way to keep track of your list and is easy to update. Some people use a binder, with a list of "cold," "warm," and "hot" potential prospects. Some maintain their list in sales tracking software. Some companies have this system built in. Me? I'm a mess. I tend to have things everywhere, and just focus on immediate follow-up and checking-in. You simply need to be organized enough for **you**! Bottom line: you and your team members need to do what works best for your individual needs to build and track your contact list. We offer different tracking tools for our team, depending on their personality and preference.

Every contact and interaction is a potential connection and lead. This doesn't mean you become a stalker and hound everyone you know to buy from you or join the business. It means you are a loud and proud network marketer who effortlessly builds relationships and maximizes connections for mutual benefit. While cultivating those relationships, if there's something you can help with, you offer it. There's no fear, no expectation, and attachment to the response.

If it works, great. If not, that's ok too.

Next, develop a strategy to contact people. Get with you mentor and go over ways to turn contacts into a revenue stream. Guaranteed, your mentor has a script that is easy to duplicate.

EFFING SIMPLE HOMEWORK

Your effing simple homework for this chapter is "easy"—start with your contact list! Develop a list of several hundred names you can invite to your event, grand opening, or ribbon cutting.

What are you waiting for? Start now!

If it helps, consider using technology to help build this—there are several great contact list programs, or you can use spreadsheets. Whatever works for you! More important than the "program" is your list. Build it, then use it!

Successful network marketers rarely retire, but it's not because they need the money. It's because they're having so much fun, and they would miss the personal and social rewards that network marketing provides.

Zig Ziglar & John Hayes

Chapter 9

Effing Simple Income Producing Activities (IPAs)

Contacts on a list don't bring income. Connecting with and serving those contacts does. That's cultivation and we do this through IPAs.

After creating a contact list, the following steps to systematic success involve IPAs. Keep in mind that every contact and connection does not equal an immediate or personal sale. However, every cultivated connection can lead to a sale (down the line or through a referral). People buy from others they know and trust. It's worth it time it takes to build and reinforce your relationship so your connections know and trust you. Also, sometimes it takes multiple contacts and exposure in different ways (personal experience, referral, testimonial, email, social media, phone) before individuals commit to your product and/or your business.

Don't let that stop you. Revisit your why.

Here are seven foolproof ways to cultivate your contacts for connection (and mutual benefit):

1. **Create Your Business Presentation**—Demonstrate a clear and compelling response to the inevitable question you encounter with every new contact—"What do you do?" Create your elevator speech and develop a clear, repeatable business presentation. (Good network marketing companies will provide this for you. It's up to you to make it your own and put it to use.)

2. **Hold Three-way Connection Calls**—Have a new partner with a great lead they aren't sure they can close? Get on the line with your partner and close the lead. Share your knowledge to achieve the sale while mentoring your partner at the same time.

   If you have a big vision for your business, then three-way connection calls are Numero Uno in my book. I built my business on three-way connection calls—as have all of the leaders in our business. Focus on those three-way connection calls with your up-line and use a script that they have used.

Quite a few people ask me what to say on a three-way connection call. Always lead with the business and if you do not have a duplicable script, then create one. The entire call should be no more than 10 minutes. The third party is the validation, especially when you are new. This will tremendously help your business, so you learn and so does your potential business partner listening to the information.

When I am talking to or messaging people to get them on a three-way connection call, it is a great way to get them there. Here is what I say:

"I'm so excited to be in this new business. It's going to be huge! I thought of you and I think that you'll be great at this. I don't know if this is the right decision for you or not, but I would love 10 minutes of your time to see to get your opinion."

If they say "No," you can respond with, "And, if it isn't, do you know of someone who would be interested?"

All you have to do is just keep it simple. I don't send a prospect anything electronically because if you can't get them on the phone, then that shows how they are going to run their business. You can't run a successful business without getting on the phone, or belly-to-belly. Your phone is worth thousands and thousands of dollars every single month. You need to make sure that you're getting as many people as you can on the phone!

Many people still do not do three-way connection calls. I must tell you that if you are not doing three-way connection calls, then your business is going to suffer and you won't be able to grow your business. Furthermore, you also cannot run a business strictly off of social media. Things can be misconceived on occasion because text does not convey. I have gotten caught up in this. Never say anything on social media that you wouldn't say to someone's face.

3. **Schedule Business Launch**—Here, you can introduce others to your products and business opportunity. These can be individualized, one-on-ones or parties/groups tailored to your network offering.

Your "Grand Opening" or "Ribbon Cutting" is the ideal way to **open** your business! Think happy hour, open house, casual and fun. Be sure to share pictures of your event on social media. Invite people you think would appreciate making some extra money, benefiting from your product or service, a cup of coffee or glass of wine, and great conversation! Also, you can do a private Facebook launch for your long distance folks before your physical one. This w2ill give you practice.

Pick a date five to seven days in advance —be careful not to schedule too far in advance. Do **not** send a Facebook or Eventbrite invite without personally speaking to a potential guest first. Here's a good opener, "I am so super excited to start a new business. Can you come to support me and give me your opinion? We'll have lots of fun, too!" Have your event somewhere cool, so people will want to show up. Offer a few drinks, carafes of wine, and a few appetizers or pastries at a coffee shop.

Now, invite people! Over invite!

Contact folks on your list using **their** preferred method of communication. If they prefer phone calls, give them a call. If they don't answer, and you leave a message, say something quick and easy like, "Hey, I have a quick question. Can you call me back?" When they respond, share the details of your business launch. If they prefer text messages, or Facebook/Instagram messaging, send them a quick note. "Hey, I have a quick question. Are you free for the next five minutes?" If they say, "yes," then call them and share your invite.

Once you are in conversation, simply tell them about the event, and follow this quick outline to get the most out of your time and efforts. First, confirm that they can make it. If they say, "Yes!" make sure they know that friends are welcome! You can ask, "Is there anyone you know who'd enjoy being a part of this?" If the answer is "No!" say a quick "Thanks," and "No worries! Let's catch up after the event. When's a good day and time?"

Keep your event easy and casual. Bring just a few products, brochures, and gifts for your guests. If you can, invite an organizational VIP, like your mentor, or someone who is very successful in the business to share their story. Starter kits are great to have on hand, and working with your mentor on your first event is also very helpful.

Don't expect too many people to sign-up on the spot. Your secret weapon after your event is your follow-up!

4. **Connect on the Fly**—Capitalize on your "out and about" time. Introduce yourself, talk to others, share samples, and promote your business everywhere you can.

You will always be looking for new clients and recruits, and the best part is you don't need to have a party, or carry the product with you to share your business. When you are passionate about something, it radiates from you. Every time I am "out and about" it's an opportunity for business, so I always try to look professional and clean to naturally expand my business opportunity. These days, connection is even easier due to social media, as people look to their peers before trying something new. However, do not start using and posting on social media until after you have officially launched your business. This is very important as it can water down your business. You can also do a private Facebook party before your launch with your long-distance contacts/friends.

When you are an entrepreneur, you're constantly working and demonstrating what people can achieve if they decide to work with you. It's a matter of presenting that model of success and connection. This doesn't mean showing off, but they should be able to visibly see your success, and how much you love the product or service that you are committed to. They should see you reflecting the success you are trying to sell, and whenever possible, it should be obvious that you use, and **love** the products you represent.

The good news is that I absolutely love what I do, and I believe in the product, so it's easy and fun for me. Sometimes it doesn't even feel like work, if you know what I mean.

I carry samples of our product with me wherever I go. I love to chat up the product. Not to push it on people, or to push the business opportunity on anyone who will listen. But, to have it available, and on-hand so that when and if the moment strikes, I'm prepared.

Again, network marketing is about building relationships and friendships, and most importantly, trust. People see and hear how much I love the product, and our opportunity. Naturally, they get curious. They ask questions, or they listen to me carrying on about this, that, or the other thing. I know it might sound silly, but that's how I am. I use my mouth, and I am always talking to people. That's just me.

In addition to samples, I also carry my business cards, brochures, and basically everything I need to conduct my business. Thank the good Lord for smart phones that make it easy to do business anywhere, anytime. You never know when opportunities for making new connections will happen, so I'm always ready. My eyes and ears are always open to whoever might be in my vicinity and might make be a valuable relationship, either directly or indirectly.

5. **Follow-Up**—Keep your leads warm by connecting with them regularly, servicing their needs, making yourself available for questions, and closing the sale. Cultivation helps you get the most of any business transaction, but it's even more true in network marketing. Keep in mind that the relationship doesn't end after the first sale or recruitment of a new network partner. You will continue to interact with the person long after they've joined you.

I'm sure you have all heard of the phrase "The fortune is in the follow-up." Everyone should consider the following points when preparing to follow-up with prospects. This is a process that tells you whether you can form a long-lasting business relationship with the prospect. Make sure you know why you are taking in a new recruit, because when you know their skills, then you can capitalize on them and put them to good use.

In this business, you sift and sort, not convince.

When first starting out, it's a good idea to have an experienced up-line or mentor to assist you with prospecting and follow-up. This will help boost your conversion rate and make you an expert within no time.

Before you drag your mentor to your next meeting, remember that a call is often as effective as an in-person meeting. Contact the prospect and let them know you intend to bring someone to the meeting. It would help if you mentioned some of the accomplishments your mentor has in the industry and encourage the prospect to ask questions. If the follow-up is done through a phone call, you can ask them to join in on the three-way connection call (most people are using Zoom for video calls).

When conducting the follow-through meeting or phone call, find out what the extra money could do for the prospect, and work from that angle. What they want is a solution to their problems. This is what you need to target when doing the follow-throughs. Find out what that extra money could do for them, and you have a decent angle to work from.

Start with, "Well, I'm calling to ask if you had chance to review the information I gave you?"

If they forgot about the information you sent, chances are they are not remotely interested in what you're selling. If, however, they made time to read the material, then you can move on to the next question. One of the concepts behind successful follow-ups is to make sure the prospect thinks about the positive aspects of the business opportunity, and whether those positive aspects are accurate or of their own interpretation.

By asking the right questions, you can steer the conversation in the right direction and have the prospect focusing on what is important— that is, the remediation of **their** immediate problems.

Ideally, you want to get back with your prospect as soon as possible, preferably within 24 hours, while the idea is still fresh on their minds. You also don't want them to talk to the wrong people and get some negative feedback about the industry. It is harder to get them past negative impressions when the feedback comes from close friends or family. Regardless, you'll find transparency builds trust—and your gut is the best indicator of what to share.

The follow-up process can take anywhere from a few days to several weeks and in some cases, you can go for months or even years building a friendship and the dream until the time comes for them to join you.

General Follow-Up Tips

- Start by building a friendship with the prospect. Do this by taking a sincere interest in their dreams, goals, and their daily life.
- Book the next follow-up at the conclusion of the plan.
- Ideally, you should follow-up within two days.
- You may do the follow-up yourself or have your sponsor assist you.
- Build them a dream. Dreams inspire people and stimulate action. Find out what their dreams area and what their immediate goals are.
- Train them. Information is very powerful.

6. **Networking Events**— Attend as many networking events you can and be sure to work the room at events. Here's where the rubber meets the road! Once you are committed to your network marketing business, you have to get out there! Find as many opportunities as you can to attend networking events. These can be business networking events like Business Network International (BNI), Chambers of Commerce, and conferences or conventions. Look on Facebook to find out about local events in your area. Ask your friends and colleagues where they recommend you go in order to network.

When you are at these events, don't try to push a sale, or push the opportunity. Instead, use your time to engage with people and listen to them. Ask about their dreams and where they want to be in life. Take a sincere interest in their lives, interests, passions, hobbies and who they are as people. As you build these friendships and relationships, you don't need to sell your business. It will sell itself.

Take the time to build relationships so people can get to know you, like you, and trust you. If the time feels right, talk to them about what you do, or invite them to an event. Keep in mind, the worst thing you can do is meet someone and see them as a "prospect that must be conquered!" Take your time; prospecting and relationship building is more like foreplay than intercourse. When people meet you, and you show them that you're trustworthy, they will naturally be curious about how you are so successful. When that happens, you can introduce them to the opportunity. They will already see that you're wildly successful, or you know people who are (if you're just getting started), and they'll want in!

Keep in mind, it can take weeks, months, and years before some prospects "seal the deal" with a commitment. Don't worry, the right relationships will turn into business. Because it was built organically it will have more lasting power as well.

7. **Rinse and Repeat**—Take the time to determine if you're getting the results you're looking for, reset as appropriate, and repeat.

When you are a network marketer or an entrepreneur, self-accountability is your best friend. Part of being "self-accountable" is knowing when you are making excuses. Are you making excuses **or** are you getting yourself into activity? Are you complaining instead of changing? Only you can change your current situation. On average, it takes between five and seven years to be really successful in network marketing—it's a lot of work! And, you have to stick to it, avoiding switching from company, to company, to company. Longevity is key to success, so choose carefully.

When people come to me who feel stuck because they had a roller coaster month or they are not meeting their goals, I tell them to "Use this down time." This is the time to concentrate on income-producing activities and personal activity. This will help your business going forward. You can't build a business on a few people or a couple of leader legs. It won't work! Also, to make sure you navigate the tough times, have an upline or accountability partner you can vent to (only when needed), bounce ideas off of, and to keep you in check.

When you are building a network marketing business, a good goal is to promote a new member to your downline every quarter **and** build a new team every quarter. Stay busy!

Rewards and recognition are key to continuing momentum. The process of highlighting your teammates' achievements helps to build respect as your prospect learns more about your supportive network. You also continue to learn from your mentor, and this can help you as you grow in your business.

Don't Forget About the Advantages of Network Marketing Organizations

Joining a network marketing organization is like plugging into a huge power source. They have training, supporters, systems, and mentors in place to help you generate the success you desire. They've also tried a few things that didn't work, readjusted, and created new best practices for success.

In the same way network marketing organizations count on you for their success, don't forget to count on them for your success.

Your leader and network marketing organization are invested in your success. They will help you spread magic!

The best way to find yourself is to lose yourself
in the service of others.
Mahatma Gandhi

Chapter 10

Effing Simple Servant Leadership

We have many great examples of servant leaders in our world, including those who are no longer with us—like Mother Teresa, Princess Diana and Martin Luther King Jr. These women gave with no expectation or specific goal in mind, but to simply be helpful to others. Servant leaders always put people first, and are first and foremost, they are humanitarians. How we serve others is by putting their needs first.

My "Why" has changed so many times over the years- as you recall I got involved for the money but quickly what I have found out about money is that it is just a nice side effect. Working in network marketing is truly an opportunity to help other people reach their successes and watch them develop into servant leaders. That is what leaders do, we serve!

Now, I can see the wonderful things money can do. Money is energy, money helps, money makes more money. I **know** I can make the money. The reason I know this: I have an abundant mindset. I expect money to come and to come easily and effortlessly. People get paid what they think they are worth. It brings me joy knowing I can support others. Through this business, I'm able to show people how to not only find wealth, but do it even better than I did.

Wealth and abundance is not just about money and material things. Wealth is represented in the quality of your relationships. You demonstrate and earn wealth when you're living your life in alignment with your highest purpose. Wealth can mean being healthy, and feeling vital and important to someone. Wealth consists of pillars that include faith, family, friends, fitness, and finances. When we overemphasize one of these pillars over the others, we build something that's not stable.

For example, if you don't have one of those pillars, like health, for example, you don't have anything. If one of those pillars is missing in your life, it means that you're not being a servant leader for yourself and minding those things in your life you need to be minding on a daily basis.

Reach out to people and really love them. You can always bring in education and a certain skill set, but when you focus on what you can do for others through love, it opens so many doors. It helps develop close bonds with other people; so they trust you explicitly.

I feel like it's my obligation to share what I know about network marketing, and how it can improve the lives of those around me. I serve my team in an honest, caring way. With network marketing and my help, they can avoid foreclosure, or having a car repossessed, and afford to buy the things they need for their family to not only survive, but thrive. I love to be in service in this way. It's a wonderful honor.

When you have an inherent need to help others, it can only serve you in the long run. It creates good karma, which always comes back. You always hear stories about paying it forward. It can be as simple as letting a man behind you with two items go in front of you and your 100 items at the grocery store. Small actions like this create positivity. We are rich in love, connections, opportunities, and vision. We are blessed beyond measure. Success, wealth, and blessings are meant to be shared. We make an effort to pay our blessings forward in our community and the larger collective. To that end, we created our own non-profit (Low Country Love) to make sharing our blessings direct and meaningful.

Jay and I give back to the community through supporting domestic violence shelters, homeless shelters, and other beneficial programs. For example, very recently, one of our business organization leaders lost her home, cars, and everything to a fire. We created a fundraiser for her, requested contributions to that fund, gave the money to her directly, and created a spiritual wealth for all who donated.

I am all about the Universe; creating love, and creating joy because this joy one of the things that we can give away free. There is plenty to go around. Abundance is real; being grateful is real! I believe Jay and I are creating a legacy business. The abundance we generate will last long beyond our lives here on earth.

The power of love, without a doubt, is a fact! The power of love is what makes everything go around; it moves mountains. I will challenge you to be grateful every day. Practice it every day; all day. Get up, fill love in your heart and body; it radiates from your soul and is shared with everyone you encounter.

I think love is where my belief and faith comes from. For a long time, I didn't tap into a specific belief, and although I am not religious, I do believe there is a higher power. That power is energy—and energy is love. Until Jay helped me understand the true strength in true love, for ourselves, for each other, and for others, I'm not sure I was living my full potential. Jay taught me to love unconditionally. We share that with our children and they reflect that back to us.

When you do things from a place of authentic love, you can do no wrong. When you're coming from a place that moves you—physically, emotionally and spiritually—that's how we're supposed to live. Sadly, we're often we're told to withhold love. I shout from the rooftops, all the time, how much I love my husband, my family, and my business. Guess what? I mean it. We would not be here where we are today, without all the people who came along and made life better. If the people you interact with don't make you better, they still help you by showing you what you **don't** want to become.

Next, leaders need to be responsible for their finances. Mind your money and pay your damn taxes. When you are proud of your earnings and accomplishments (without flaunting it), your team will look up to you. They will mirror you, and they will work harder. But, remember they always work harder for praise. Acknowledge your team and the members who go above and beyond for you, the team, and their customers.

Leaders give—and give like no one's business. Your time and your love are the most significant gifts you can share with others. You will be amazed at what happens when you give selflessly. It is called being a "servant leader." Own this title. Live it. Breathe it. Do not be afraid. Fear was initially instilled in us to keep us safe from predators, and from walking off a cliff.

Fear was designed to protect us, but we have created a fear of every damn thing. Stop it now. Stop creating bullshit in your own head. Get over it, you won't die. Honestly, evaluate and ask, "What is the worst that could happen?" We

121

are safer than ever physically. Our worst fears are usually related to doubt and insecurities. Leaders must break away from fear and streamline confidence and reassurance that everything will work, when you do the work. I think a lot of people are afraid of being successful. It means more responsibility, and more work.

If this bothers you, there is a reason. Explore that reason, don't lash out at me for being raw, and serving the truth. Deal with your insecurities, deal with your shortcomings, and get over it. Instead of doubting, do something to improve your situation. Do you know why people get pissed? It's because they lead a life of mediocrity. It's so easy to just half-ass life. Make it full-assed. Get a J Lo booty when it comes to facing your fears! Go out and seize the world. That is what this book is about. Own it. Live it. Love it.

Being a servant leader doesn't mean you let people walk all over you. Stop it. I am the poster child for being too nice. When you are too nice, you are weak. Stand your ground. Don't be a pushover (I would totally use the other p word here if I thought it would offend the masses). If it feels wrong, guess what? It is wrong. Don't forget the obvious. Many of us do and kick ourselves later for ignoring all the clues. As soon as you can, engage with a CPA and business lawyer to make sure you are taking good care of your organization, and protecting yourself from issues that can, and do, come up.

Not that long ago, one of our leaders passed away. Unfortunately, she didn't have a will or trust, so her business went to her almost ex-husband. Make sure you are preserving the legacy of financial stability for the wealth that you are building. A leader takes good care of his or her business and personal assets. I could write an entire book on how you, as you build your wealth, need to protect your finances and your business. But, at the very least, acknowledge that you are not a lawyer, nor a qualified accountant, so find and hire these professionals who will look out for you, and make sure you're keeping your organization financially healthy.

Make sure you interview these professionals. Not just for their qualifications, but to determine whether your personalities mesh. Have they ever worked specifically with and for network marketing organizations? Are they aggressive at writing off things that pertain to your business? Do they know about tax credits that you have as a home-based business available in your state?

I'm taking you on your best journey ever, take the left fork in the road—the road less travelled. The road that needs paving, and the road where an undiscoverable journey will take you. There are riches you will not even know that await you. Know that I love you. I love that you are on this path of enlightenment, a journey that will give you lifelong pleasure and happiness. At the same time, you must understand this: life doesn't come without its challenges, those that make you stronger, and show you that you can beat anything. Be mindful, shut out or eliminate negativity, chatter, and gossip. You have huge opportunities in this world, as does everyone who chooses not to stay in mediocrity.

Ultimately, your family will change, and your friends will change. The people that you attract into your life will change. Accept it. Embrace it. Love it. Congratulations on your decision to be the best that you can be. Don't be afraid to move on. It will be the only way you will become who you are meant to be on your highest level! Always strive. Always be better. Always kick ass!

Let's recap on Leadership 101

- Leaders always step around the crap, not into it. They are solution driven.
- Leaders don't gossip.
- Leaders lead with integrity, honesty, and understand trustworthy relationship are priceless.
- Leaders dress and act professionally.
- Leaders "do the do" (course coming soon)! They the walk the walk. You can't expect someone to do something you won't—that is a hypocrite.
- Leaders are positive and the team's biggest cheerleader.

- Leaders lead the way and show others how to lead, not follow.
- Leaders don't quit, and they help others get through rough patches.
- Leaders are laser focused on one goal at the time, and keep the momentum going.
- Leaders don't take it personally when people don't "show up."

Now, I ask—isn't that common sense?

EFFING SIMPLE HOMEWORK

Name leaders who have been influence on you. Who are they, and how have they influenced you?

_____

_____

_____

_____

In what way are you following the Leadership 101 basics? In what ways are you not?

_____

_____

_____

_____

How do you want to help people?

_____

_____

_____

_____

How do you think helping other people helps you?

_____

_____

_____

_____

What are some "triggers" evoke fear in you? (These could be general fears, but also fears related to network marketing.)

_____

_____

_____

_____

What action steps can you take in order to alleviate fear?

_____

_____

_____

_____

Network marketing is a real-world business school for people who want to learn the real-world skills of an entrepreneur, rather than the skills of an employee.

Robert Kiyosaki

Chapter 11

Effing Simple Profession

Network marketing is hotter than ever because of some key factors that include industry growth, social proof, and consumer awareness. Along with the above, people are reawakening to the fact that there is a better way to create a higher level of income—a way that allows them to build an income around their passions, rather than balancing their passions around their time.

I love what I do, more than anything else. Believe it or not, it took me 34 years to figure it out. That's okay. Sometimes it takes that long—or longer. Whereas my 11-year-old has known what she has wanted to do since she was 8…casting call anyone?

The thing is, you have to be passionate. If you have passion for something that is your God's path, it's essential for you to pursue it.

I truly believe network marketing is the most powerful profession there is. Here is why: You can touch so many people, with limited resources and a reasonable amount of time and turn it around to a multi-million-dollar business. I mean look at us. We literally scraped together $400 to get started, and now we appreciate a multiple-eight figure income and seven revenue streams. What's better is we're not the only ones doing this. It's truly possible for everyone. In an ever-expanding world, where we have access to every piece of geography with the click of the finger, we can no longer ignore the opportunity to build.

The world has become much smaller with support technology growing in quality and availability. From anywhere, at any time, you can use technological platforms such as Zoom, GoToMeeting or SKYPE. You have to trust me here; nothing replaces face to face contact, a personal phone call, or hand-written note.

When you run your own business, you can set your schedule and work efficiently. You can walk away from your business for a month and still make money. People buy from people they trust. And, in today's world, social media allows you to build trust online where people are already looking. However, don't let technology take you away from business building activities. Instead, allow it to amplify the foundation you built.

The world is waking up. We are no longer in a world where we can get by focusing on what we want without looking to help others. As Zig Ziglar says, "You will get all you want in life, if you help enough other people get what they want." There is never a more important time to understand this principle more than now. In Network Marketing, our success is measured in the success of others. So, what are you doing to help those people who look up to you?

Build your customer base, but more importantly provide excellent customer service. Not just great service, but Bad Ass Customer Service (BACS). Your customers are the lifeblood of your business. Without customers, there is no volume. Consumable products are hotter than ever! Work with companies that have amazing products you love. When a product is aligned with emotion and you share with it joy, customers become buyers for life.

Get both feet focused on what you want from your business. I have said this time and time again—building a business is no different than a health routine; you need to stick to it and not procrastinate. In the same way you go to the gym, do yoga, go for a run—go to networking events, reach out, make your phone calls, and follow-up on business leads. When you make the one thing the **one thing**, you're going to see how your business just keeps growing. When you have divided attention, it just doesn't work. You need to go 12-wide, and 12-deep on your leadership team for lifelong residual income. And, until you do, keep that laser focus. From there, you can develop multiple streams of income, which are critical insurance policies to have. However, it's imperative to stay super focused on one thing at a time.

Bottom line, place value on your time. When you manage your business with a laser beam focus, both feet on the floor, whole body, and 110% commitment—you **will** get the results you want!

EFFING SIMPLE HOMEWORK

When you think of your "Why," does it align with your current profession and life goals?

_____

_____

_____

_____

What experience with previous professions do you have, and how might they help you succeed in network marketing?

_____

_____

_____

_____

What strategies can you use to stay laser focused?

_____

_____

_____

_____

The best marketing strategy ever: CARE.

Gary Vaynerchuk

Chapter 12

Effing Simple Social Media

Social media can be used to enhance your relationships and increase sales. Notice, I said "enhance," not "replace." You simply cannot achieve maximum success—in any business—without the personal connection.

However, social media is an amazing tool that enables you to create and build connections with those not in your current vicinity for personal meetings. Plus, technology like email campaigns, contact management systems, and customer tracking completed by good network marketing organizations enable you to maximize every personal and virtual connection achieved.

Here's the thing, word of mouth is the best referral for every network marketing team. Repeated post shares on social media about the latest movies, music, and political mishaps represent word of mouth referring (aka network marketing). Thousands of people in your network are discussing the latest movies, music, and political mishaps. Here's the money question.

Did you get paid for the recommendation that came so naturally for you?

Nope.

When you enjoy something, naturally you want to tell others about your experience and help them have the same enjoyable experience. I'm not going to say watching the latest box office hit and the aftermath is always an enjoyable experience—I'll leave that for you to judge.

But the concept remains. When you enjoy a product or service, it's natural to share it with others. Network marketing enables you to do what comes naturally, while profiting at the same time. It doesn't have to be "salesy," nor does it feel like "selling" when it's done right.

A great networker is always talking and sharing. They share themselves, their ideas, and the love. Sometimes, they do all of that while sharing a network marketing product during their "work week" to advance the brand and its products. That includes small talk and riding the "viral wave" when it's appropriate. In a digital world, the new normal is twenty-to-a-hundred personal data points a day.

Networking within social media platforms can often be a form of roulette that professionals are not only playing blindly, but failing at in almost every round, hoping for the best.

There's another way.

Beat the anxiety of "constantly pitching" and start building that network in a real way.

Everyone is in the thick of it: a pitch here, an advertisement there. Maybe a boost on a post that looks great and is doing well, but, let's face it—everyone is promoting ads that not many really want to see. Flash sales and specials should be rare.

Instead of sending a message or a pitch, tell a story of a before and after; tell a story of somebody that had success in this business; best of all, show and tell your story.

As someone who gets pitched at least 10 to 20 times a week online, I can tell you that that unsolicited pitches on social are awful, especially when it's my specific request for that kind of thing not to happen.

The reason why I avoid those pitches? They don't work because it's clear the person isn't interested in me, they are just trying to sell me something. I can spot that shit from a mile away.

Prospective clients aren't "marks" like in some con game to get as many people in the ranks as possible. Real, genuine network marketing isn't a con game. It's a company of integrity built on real relationships and constant conversations that may never equal a sale. Once a real connection is made, follow up with an offer. If they're not interested, that's okay.

Since we live on social media, there should be a "no spam" rule for every serious network marketer and team member. That's it. Instead of spam, go for the real genuine connection. It wins every time—regardless of whether or not there's a sale.

Your team will thank you, your brand will thank you, and your tribe and team will be all the better for it.

That word of mouth referral? It's going to go farther than any direct mail or email chain. That quick conversation or push of the Like-button? These things can and will connect a new team within every personal network, and for network marketers, there is no limit. The brand or business might not go viral, but if the owner or team leader is part of the brand (and they always are), new and deeper levels are made when "friends of friends" get together.

Even better, those friends become family who experience great things like travel, personal development, team success, and personal wealth together. There's nothing better than that.

In network marketing, the whole point is not to sell a product but to build a network, an army of people who are all representing that same product or service to share with others.

Robert Kiyosaki

Chapter 13

Effing Simple Product

What is your product? Do you know the fine details? Zero in on one or two things you know about the product and focus on that. The product will to open a conversation, but you need to turn that product conversation into a business conversation.

Sales in network marketing begin with products you love and prospects can buy into. Regardless of the product or industry type, you must be your own best customer. Don't use some other product (that is being a hypocrite). Begin with basic knowledge you can build on. Learning the product lines is awesome, but keep it simple. If the company has a wider product range, just focus on a few of them.

You need to provide your customers with a good reason to stay in touch with you. When selling an exceptional product your customer cannot find elsewhere, know what is special about your product and what makes it unique so you can use highlight the product and busniess advantages.

Often times, I get asked how I chose the company I am partnering with and how I choose a leader. For me, products and leadership go hand-in-hand. When you are choosing a company, there are so many facets to consider. Don't think emotionally, based on the fact you love that person or the product line. Be sure you don't make a decision without really doing your research. Use a checklist to ensure you're getting the details you need and considering all facets of the decision. I've created a checklist to evaluate network marketing organizations. You can download it at www.soeffingsimple.com.

You can get a lot of information through Direct Selling Association (DSA) which can be found at www.dsa.org. Scour the professional articles that have been written, not just opinions of a few people. You cannot believe everything you read on the internet, but there are trustworthy and reputable sources.

The DSA recently published an article on why companies fail, and what they said was spot-on. According to the DSA, the number one reason is companies lose focus on their people is a lack of focus and attention on their people.

The people working in the field are the most important commodity for a company not the product. The product should stand out in a sea of thousands. When looking for a company, the team must be the primary focus. The second area of focus should be their niche in the market.

Great programs and useful training are imperative to making connections and moving product. Make sure you have passion for the product line and focus on what sets it apart from anything else out there. In my opinion, the compensation plan should have a very generous pay-out. Comp plans that are shallow, or where you have break-away will severely affect pay checks across the board. These aspects do not create a long-term productive team or sustainable business. A company flat-out must pay their people well—and pay their people on time. And they should always be investing in their people through trainings and incentive trips.

It is very important if a company is a start-up or newer, that they have capital coupled with zero debt. Since I have been through two company closings, I can tell you, there are things to look for and things to avoid. You cannot start a direct-sales company (or any company) on a wing and a prayer. It must be efficient, planned out, and have backing— whether is the funds are their own or someone else's. At the same time, be wary of investors because this may inhibit the creativity of the owners. Creativity and expansion are critical.

If someone else's money is funding the organization, make sure the owners have full execution of decisions.

Trust your instinct and intuition. If something feels off or not right, that is exactly what it is. If it is meant to be, you will know in your deepest self. That is how I knew I found the right company. It just felt natural and blossomed from the beginning. If it doesn't feel right, and you push forward, you will come across as disingenuous and struggle.

What are the company's future plans? They should be talking about this on business opportunity calls. Is expansion a priority? Incentives like a car program, travel, free product and jewelry. are also part of what you should consider. A recognition program is important because people want and need praise. Some companies won't have any of these, but they will have cash bonuses. This is the company investing in you, so take advantage of these programs, and recognize companies that do this for their people; investing in their leadership.

What kind of getting started or fast track program do they have? That is when a new consultant gets started, and the company gives them a period of time to earn extra money, product, or both. Is there a cap to the compensation plan? This means is there a cut-off to making a certain amount of money. Do they have very clear policies and procedures?

You need to be self-sufficient, and have your own training materials if your company does not provide them. A company may have many materials, but as a leader, it's important to share your own style. Aligning yourself with a good leader or a good team is important. Successful teams have a system in place that is duplicatable—they can show you and teach you step-by-step how to do what they did so you can do the same.

The great part about having these types of systems is that they have a tremendous trickle-down effect. People start to sponsor, and then their people start to sponsor. Even if you found out about a company through someone new, if they are plugged in and working with a leader, that leader will help you as well.

Being together in a team atmosphere and having a wealth of support is imperative. As a leader, it is important to let leaders lead and teach those they bring in so they can go and do the same exact thing.

Interview the company and its leadership. Align yourself with someone you identify with and they will welcome you checking them out to see if they are a fit. Basically, you are interviewing one another. Also, a great leader will match their time with your efforts. The work must be done by you. All a great leader can do is guide you.

Does the company sell to all segments of the population? What is their background, and who owns it? What is the owner's background? How much of a percentage are you making? Where is the rest of the money going? Are they putting it in their pocket or back into the company or to their people?

You know that you have a good business by looking at their people, the products and pay checks of team members. It can be hard to find something unique. For example, just look how many jewelry or skincare companies there are. I highly recommend a consumable product; something that the customer will need more of. People are the commodity. **You** are the commodity.

We are dream builders and problem solvers. These are the things to look for when picking a direct sales company to work with. Give everything you can to build your new business. No excuses! Don't use your children as an excuse. Use them as the reason! Remember your "Why," and find a way; because you're either going to find a way or find an excuse.

EFFING SIMPLE HOMEWORK

Use the checklist found at www.soeffingsimple.com to review either your current network marketing company, or another network marketing company you are considering aligning with. What new information did you find out?

_____

_____

_____

_____

_____

Network marketing tends to develop the type of leader who influences others by being a great teacher, teaching others to fulfill their life's dreams by teaching others to go for their dreams.

Robert Kiyosaki

Chapter 14

Effing Simple Training

One of the most important things you can do in your Direct Selling business is to plug into training calls, host team calls, and attend company events. Everyone on your team is plugged into the same system and the same network marketing training, which enables every person to get the same information.

You have 90 days or less to teach someone the ins and outs of this business. Become an expert at the onboarding procedures you receive when you sign-up. Our Success Starters Guide—located at www.tonivans.com—will give you a jump start.

If you want a huge, successful team of distributors that is duplicatable, then every person must plug into the network marketing training. Organizational training provides the support you need to have financial freedom. Whether it is calls, social medial, email, or an online office forum, there must be outreach and communication with representatives, current and prospective customers. If your team members are not getting the necessary information, then you will end up with a high maintenance, low productivity team. Keep in mind that it is their responsibility to show up, and your responsibility to offer comprehensive training in several different ways.

For training, keep it simple and ensure your people can duplicate it. This is how you sustain a business, create residual income, and you draw other people into your business. A confused mind says "No." It is like spinning plates on a stick. You can get five plates spinning, and when one of them starts to wobble because they need your help with prospects or closing, then you can give them some attention and keep their plate spinning. Some of your plates might need more work than others, but you still have to work to make sure all of them are spinning well.

Hint: Stop trying to drag your people across the finish line. If they are not reaching out to you or contact you for help, then let it go—I call this "Bless and Release." Give them your blessing and move on. But, for your active team members, get them into activity and make sure they are on task to create and build momentum!

Network marketing is a team sport! However, success beings with **you**. You must be plugged in if you expect your team to be plugged in. When everyone is on the same page, they are receiving the same information and moving in the same direction, in the same way, and at the same time. National and regional company conferences are held for a reason—to inspire, connect, and motivate the team. You need to be there. That clichéd saying "Showing up is going up," absolutely holds merit. If you don't have anyone locally conducting team meetings, start your own. You have to show your team you care, and more importantly, demonstrate that you are committed. You team will follow your lead. Here is the thing—this won't kill you. If you truly want change, you will follow the guide given here. Most people won't give it 100% effort and that is why they fail. It isn't anything else but their own lack of commitment.

Dedicate your time and efforts to your committed downlines. You need to be there for your downline and ready to guide them through the process of generating leads to build and develop their own networks. Teach a very clear and specific system. Remember that duplication is all about providing team members with the methods which you yourself have used with success. Your methods are proven to be effective.

Set aside 10% of your earnings to invest in your team. Take another 10% of your earnings for travel expenses to visit your team members; either individually or as a group. These efforts will go a long way to building a powerful, self-sustaining income-generating team. A word of caution: make sure you have an expected Return on Investment (ROI) for every investment. If you travel and you are not getting in front of new people with your team, that is a waste of time and money.

Develop training programs for team members to adopt. They should be created for your team to perform the very same methods themselves and then train others following your example. Training is only one part of the puzzle though. You must hold team members accountable for their performance. You take time teaching them the system and this includes making sure that your downlines follow it accordingly. Be firm, but never overbearing, and encourage them by helping them understand how well the system works if the methods are performed according to the duplicatable system. Stress the process so they can enjoy its fruits as you do.

Identify the leaders and raise them up. Recognition is the mother of this industry. The nature of this is all about raising oneself to help others raise themselves and to help even more to do the same. It is very important to recognize the leaders in your network and develop them further.

Encourage these people to keep shining brighter and you will have built a stronger relationship that is lasting and vital to your future growth.

RINSE AND REPEAT OVER AND OVER!

EFFING SIMPLE HOMEWORK

Visit www.tonivans.com and click on the Toolkit link. Watch the Onboarding 101 video, and check out the other resources.

What kinds of training do you think would be helpful as you start your new business?

_____

_____

_____

_____

What types of training and support will you offer your team?

_____

_____

_____

_____

What reproducible training materials are already available from your company?

_____

_____

_____

_____

What types of materials might you want to develop to enhance your effectiveness as a leader?

_____

_____

_____

_____

How will you recognize and reward members of your team when they make certain levels?

_____

_____

_____

_____

Effective network marketing is discipline,
carrying out your vision,
doing what you commit to do.

Stephen Covey

Chapter 15

Effing Simple Presentation

Presentation isn't just the way you present your company or its products. Presentation is the whole package of who you are and the business you represent. This includes dressing the part, and acting the part of an accomplished network marketing professional. You are, in a sense, your own business card. I can't stress this enough brand yourself.

Often in network marketing, people brand the company or product without thinking about branding themselves—**huge mistake.** You are the one that creates the experience. It's important to remember, you are the one people buy from. Align yourself with a great company and a great product, but at the end of the day, people buy from people they know, like, and trust. Don't ever forget this. You can generate greater success when you provide the best customer service and experience. Successful network marketing involves high touch customer service.

Power is a great word. Just like money, wealth, success, and tithing—when done in the spirit of service. People will do business with you if they like and trust you. To help cultivate trust, you need to look and act professional at all times. Dress the part—in a way that makes you feel powerful. For some, that's business casual. For others, it's full blown professional. Others feel more at home in jeans or shorts.

The most important part of dressing "professionally" is being comfortable—I don't mean yoga pants or pajama comfortable—but dressing in a way that lets your personality shine. Clothes are only part of the equation. Your body language matters too. Standing in the Wonder Woman or Captain America stance is a powerful visual that sets your intention. Stand with your legs apart, look up with your arms pointed out and open. I do this every time before I speak to remind myself how valuable what we have is.

Remember, this is your business, your career, and your livelihood. Always have business cards on hand, make the appointment when you meet, and always know your next two appointments. Your smile and disposition is the biggest part of your profession. When out and about, be a positive person with joyous energy and look to interact with people who reflect the same. You want to meet people who have great presence. I choose limit my interaction with anyone that has a negative energy, and sometimes I've found that although I can fill their need, people with negative energy are not interested. They do not want to hear about things that will take them out of their comfort zone. More importantly, they don't want to do the things that change their lives.

Selling is about creating and building relationships. Sometimes they build quickly, and other times it takes years to build. Some will be negative, some will be mean, some are amazing, some productive—regardless, never let anything slow you down.

Power prospecting means you need that 30 and 60 second elevator speech that is something people can remember you by. Have fun with this and come up with something catchy. You need to impress in seven seconds or less. What is an elevator pitch? A pitch is a concise "teaser" of your life laced with clues on who you are and what you do. It's used to generate enough interest and intrigue so others want to know more about and what you do, all in the time it takes to ride an elevator—say, 30 seconds to two minutes.

What is your opening line? What is the beginning of your story? Here are some possible examples:

- "I work for the kind of company where everyone is rewarded for their contributions and not their title."

- "I spend my time helping others earn an extra $500 a month by becoming sharers and givers."
- "I love working out just as much as I love mixing up a delicious protein shake afterward for recovery."

KISS: Keep It Simple Silly!

However, you begin or end, remember to keep it simple. When sharing the joy of what you do, what your life is like, and where you are now, the script needs to sound seamless. Use words and phrases that elicit interest from your prospect. Simplify your message and confidently broadcast how fun and easy a network marketing business can be. And much like you began, you will want to end with an intriguing cliff-hanger to prompt a response. For example, "I spend my time helping others earn an extra $500 a month or more by becoming sharers and givers. It's truly been one of the most rewarding things I've ever done. Plus, the products we share are incredible. I started doing it part-time two years ago, and I never looked back. It is something that has given me the opportunity to pursue my passion and have extra time to spend with my family."

I tend to not spend a ton of time describing the product. I might spend three minutes during a presentation, or just a few words during my elevator speech. I provide links and information on the product, but I tend to highlight just a few things that will help more than 90% of individuals out there, or just focus on one specific product or products that this particular person might benefit from. It's important not to overwhelm people with details. *Instead, overwhelm them with your positivity and opportunity.*

If you are presenting to a group, use PowerPoint and other technology that can get between you and your audience sparingly. When necessary, be sure to use less words and more pictures. For a guide, check out Carmine Gallo's "Talk Like Ted." I like to talk with people, not at people. I don't want them staring at a screen or away from me. And, I will keep them engaged by keeping my presentation short (no more than 21 minutes), and laser focused on what I can do to help them. Even though I have a script, I do keep it personal— it's not something I read, it's something I know, inside and out.

In a typical presentation, I follow an outline of how people can spend, save, or make money with us. Of course, I toss in some dumb jokes...because that's me! I go through the basic information of who, what, and how. Who is this for? What makes our product different? How can it help you? Finally, I ask for the sale. Most people who have a hard time recruiting new clients or members because they don't specifically close, or ask for the sale.

A simple close I use is this small ask, "Where do you see yourself? Do you see yourself spending money with us, saving money with us, or making money with us?" Boom! Those three options take the power from you and gives it to your prospect. Remember, when you are working your business, keep your mouth shut. The one that talks first loses. Most people I know (including me) interrupt...what you have to say is not more important. What the person in front of you is saying is the most important.

If you have an intriguing opening line and hook, the person you are talking to might naturally begin asking you questions. You will know by their questions that your sparkly pitch has done its job at piquing their interest, and you can naturally move toward setting up a meeting. But, if the person you are talking to doesn't respond by asking questions, you can insert a clear and concise Call to Action question at the end. For example, "Can I call or email you tonight with more information?"

Sometimes presentation meetings take the format of a group social, or an outing. I've been known to go bowling, meet at a wine and paint party, or go to a wine tasting. We mingle, get to know each other, and then conduct the business information. There's always time for more fun after we talk business. I want people to really see and feel our organizational culture. I'm the type of person who wants to have fun, so I want to make sure prospective recruits and customers feel and see that when I interact with them. Also, fun brings joy and people want to be a part of a community that's joyful—Although most of them don't even know that yet.

For some events, I'll bring in motivational speakers for our team. These speakers are people completely unrelated to network marketing with a good story to tell. One of the best meetings we ever had was when we brought in a former Navy Seal to speak about how he helps wounded veterans. He talked about his journey, serving, and almost dying twice in Iraq. He masterfully equated the importance of teamwork to survival of your entire platoon. This is the same for dreams, and living your true purpose, including challenges and stresses that go along with that journey.

Even when we feel like giving up, as he almost did by putting a gun into his mouth pulling the trigger, there's always a reason to soldier on. He was lucky. The gun didn't fire (the crazy thing was, he had fired that gun hundreds of times without fail). Through this, he realized he was given a second chance and he woke up so he could help and support the people in his life who love him and others that were suffering from Post-Traumatic Stress Disorder (PTSD). At this time, he knew he had to be a true leader. He quit drugs and alcohol overnight because his calling was to lead. There wasn't a dry eye in the house that day. Andrew, thank you for changing every single person that hears your story.

Nothing is more powerful than watching yourself in action. Create a real-life situation and set up your phone or camera and record yourself giving your elevator speech to a friend or spouse. Then replay the recording and watch yourself in action and visually see what you may need to improve upon.

- Do you talk too much with your hands?
- Do you avoid making eye contact?
- Do you tend to sway back and forth when you talk?
- Do you sound overly excited or passionate?
- Do you sound monotone?

To polish it up even more, get feedback by asking your up-line to hear your speech. They may be able to offer some small tweaks that provide amazing results.

EFFING SIMPLE HOMEWORK

Let's write an "elevator speech!" Follow these steps: Observe, Care, Cater

1. Observe: You must always assume the person wants to know "what is in it for me." First, observe their dress, their eyes, their facial expressions, what they are holding and other parts of their character. What is unique about them? What is their energy like?
2. Care: As you are observing them, do so without judgment or scrutiny.
3. Cater: Cater to your first question. After you have consciously done the first two steps, you should be able to easily tailor your question toward the individual. Here are some examples: "That's a nice suit, what do you do for a living?" "Looks like you are headed to the gym; where do you go?"

Be genuinely interested in them. When they inevitably ask about you, you'll be ready when you develop your opening line—Mine is "I get paid to wash my hair!"

Think of some opening lines that will keep the conversation going:

_____

_____

_____

_____

What is part of your story that you can introduce in a fun way. For example, "It was the best of times, it was the worst of times…" then tell your story.

_____

_____

_____

_____

What is it that you do? Don't forget to reference your "Why!"

_____

_____

_____

_____

Piece the above together to try out a couple of "elevator speeches." Share them with trusted people who will give you honest feedback and input. What changes do you need to make?

_____

_____

_____

_____

_____

_____

_____

_____

_____

_____

_____

_____

_____

_____

_____

_____

The only way to do great work is to love what you do.
If you haven't found it yet, keep looking.
Don't settle. As with all matters of the heart,
you'll know when you've found it.

Steve Jobs

Maybe you are one of those I am going to read the back page first. So here are my top tips:

- *Lead by example*
- *Dress and act professionally*
- *Be duplicatable*
- *Personally and professionally develop everyday*
- *Get moving (exercise is necessary)*
- *Be a servant*
- *Be humble*
- *Be knowledgeable*
- ***MOST IMPORTANTLY, HAVE FUN!!!***

KEEP IT EFFING SIMPLE
~TONI